Shipwrecked at the Library

and other exploits

Written by
ALEXA TEWKESBURY
Illustrated by
ANNA-MARIA GLOVER

kevin mayhew

kevin
mayhew

First Published in 2023 by Kevin Mayhew Ltd

Kevin Mayhew Ltd
Fengate Farm
Rattlesden
Bury St Edmunds
Suffolk
IP30 0SZ

Sparky Smart written by Alexa Tewkesbury
Illustrated by Anna-Maria Glover

ISBN 9781838581534
Product code: 1501726

Meet the family!

Sparky (Sabrina)

Mr Smart (Seb/Dad)

Mrs Smart (Stella/Mum)

Stanley

Sissy

THE BAGGS

Auntie Bella (Stella's twin sister)
The twins: Nat and Archie (aka 'the crinkly cousins')
Grandad Bagg (Stella and Auntie Bella's dad)

RESIDENTS OF PRIORY PARK

Miss Clatworthy
Her cats:
Monday, Tuesday
and Thursday

The Obis
Mr Obi
Mrs Obi
Baby Eric
Minnie,
the Chihuahua

Shipwrecked at the library

Today, Sparky thought, had been just about normal. Well, as normal a day as was possible in the Smarts' house on Priory Park.

Mr Smart had gone to work in the morning. That was normal. What wasn't quite so normal was that he'd put on his brand-new shorts before leaving the house.

Mr Smart worked as a personal trainer and helped people to get fit. Usually, he changed into his personal training kit when he arrived at the gym. But not today. Because of the newness of his shorts, he thought they could do with a bit of wearing-in before he did any exercise in them. So today, he'd decided to wear them to drive to work.

As normal, Sparky had walked to school with Grandad Bagg that morning. Also as normal, Mrs Smart had taken Sparky's brother, Stanley, to school in the car. On the way, she'd dropped little Sissy off at the childminder.

It was a Monday, which meant Sissy would be with the childminder all day. Normally on a Monday when Mrs Smart picked Sissy up at the end of the afternoon, Sissy would be grizzly. What wasn't normal today was that Sissy was grizzly from the moment she woke up.

Once Mrs Smart had dropped Stanley and Sissy off, as normal, she had headed for school herself. She wasn't looking forward to her day of maths teaching. She'd complained (as normal) at breakfast that it had already been a very long term and the last thing she needed was more homework to mark. What wasn't quite as normal as – well – normal, was that as Mrs Smart parked her car, gathered her bags and walked into school, she wasn't late.

But the thing was, Sparky often thought, if absolutely *everything* was normal and nothing was *un*-normal at all – for the Smarts, that simply wouldn't be normal.

'What's all this?' asked Grandad.

He and Sparky were enjoying a quiet after-school sticky bun in the kitchen when Mrs Smart burst in through the front door. She was followed by a gloomy-looking Stanley and a grizzly Sissy with a screwed-up face. (In fact, Mrs Smart wasn't so much followed by Sissy as having to hoick her along. The littlest Smart clung to her mum's right leg and refused to let go. Not even when Mrs Smart tripped up the front step and only just managed to save herself from sprawling headlong across the hall carpet.)

'What a lot of noise, Missy Sissy!' Grandad appeared in the kitchen doorway. 'Your sister and I were just enjoying a quiet after-school sticky bun.'

Sissy's face crumpled further still. She held on to Mrs Smart's leg more tightly, threw back her head and wailed, 'I wanna sticky bum! I WANNA STICKY BUM!'

At the kitchen table, Sparky continued to munch her bun. Yes, as Mondays went, this one, on the whole, was quite normal.

It continued to be normal, too, right up until ten minutes after Grandad had left for the community centre. Monday evenings were one of the times when he taught his crochet class.

'My library books!'

The squeal came from Sparky's bedroom. The squealer was Sparky.

The next moment, Sparky shot through the doorway, hurtled along the landing and down the stairs.

Stanley was at the foot of the staircase, about to head up to his bedroom. Fortunately, hurtling is quite noisy. So he had plenty of time to realise the danger he was in and stand sensibly to one side.

'Mum!' Sparky yelled and threw herself into the kitchen. 'My library books!'

Mrs Smart was sitting down, trying to enjoy a large mug of tea. It stood on the table in front of her and looked hot and inviting. But Sissy kept grabbing at her hands and squirming in her lap. And Mrs Smart was beginning to realise that drinking it would be impossible.

She let out a deep sigh, as if someone had jumped on her chest and forced all the air out. 'You don't have to yell, Sparky. I'm worn to a frazzle today as it is, I don't need yelling at.'

'But, Mum, my library books!'

'Yes?' Mrs Smart turned to look at Sparky with tired, tea-thirsty eyes. 'What about your library books?'

'They're due back – today!'

'Today?' Once again, an invisible someone jumped on Mrs Smart's chest. 'Well, why didn't you say so before now? Why didn't you warn me last week? I can't be expected to remember everything, you know. I'm in the middle of a *very* long term. I mean, this is hopeless. I dread to think how many library fines we've had to pay because of your overdue books and now we'll have to pay another one.'

'No!' Sparky shook her head. 'No, we have to take them

back today. Now! I promised that librarian lady last time that I'd never take my books back late again. And I can't break my promise, I just can't.'

Mrs Smart gazed longingly at her mug of tea. 'Well, I'm sorry, Sparky, but we can't possibly go to the library now. It's too late. I think Sissy must be coming down with a cold or something. She won't stop whinging. I'm not dragging her out again. It's wet and horrible out there.'

'But I promised!' Sparky's voice was desperate.

Mrs Smart rolled her eyes. 'Then you shouldn't have done. Either that, or you should have written a big note to yourself so you didn't forget until it was too late.'

Sparky shook her head again. 'But it's *not* too late. The library doesn't close until half past six.'

'No, Sparky,' said Mrs Smart. 'I'm not going out again now. I want to get Sissy all ready for an early night. I'm sorry, but no.'

'But –'

'No!'

As Mrs Smart's 'No!' exploded out of her mouth, Sissy twisted in her lap and caught the longed-for mug of tea with her elbow. The mug tipped over on the table with a light 'clunk'. Tea spewed in all directions.

A second 'No!' screeched its way out of Mrs Smart's mouth.

'I've got it!' said Sparky. She grabbed a cloth and began to mop up the spill. Sadly, she couldn't save Sissy's pinafore dress or Mrs Smart's trousers. Happily, Mrs Smart had been waiting so long to enjoy her tea that it was now only lukewarm.

'I know!' Sparky said suddenly, clutching the cloth mid mop. Her face beamed. Sparky was well known for her quick thinking and bright ideas, but sometimes she surprised even herself. 'You don't need to take me to the library at all. I can go on the bus. With Stanley.'

When any of the Smarts mentioned Stanley's name, Stanley seemed to know. Even when he was in another part of the house and it was just about impossible that he could have heard. Sometimes, even when he wasn't in the house at all...

'Not with me!' Stanley called from his bedroom upstairs. 'I'm not going anywhere on the bus. I've got homework to do. I have got a life, you know.'

'Oh, *please*, Mum?'

As Sparky had stopped mopping, the tea had begun to dribble off the table once more. This time, it ran onto Sissy's white socks. Sissy stopped whinging for a moment to watch the spreading brown stains.

'The bus stops right outside the library and I did promise. You wouldn't want me to break a promise, would you?'

Mrs Smart pressed her lips into a hard, straight line. 'Fine,' she huffed at last. 'But only if Stanley goes with you and only if you make another promise: that you'll go straight there and come straight back.'

'I'm not going anywhere,' called Stanley. 'You can't make me!'

'Jolly good,' said Mrs Smart. She eased herself out of her seat and, holding a wet Sissy slightly away from her, walked damply out of the kitchen.

'You're to drop the books off with Sparky and come right back home, Stanley,' said Mrs Smart as she made her way upstairs.

'I'm not going.'

'And don't forget to take your mobile. I'm not having the two of you out and about on your own without a phone.'

'Own widout a bone,' whinged Sissy.

Stanley's wasn't the grumpiest face on the bus. That belonged to the bus driver.

'I'm sorry but we don't have any change,' Sparky said as she held out a £20 note.

The driver looked at it without taking it. 'And what am I supposed to do with that?' she growled.

'Erm...' Sparky was a little taken aback. When you travelled on the bus, you paid a fare. She'd never really considered what the bus driver did with it.

'Well...' she went on, 'you've probably been doing a lot of driving around today already. So perhaps you could use it to buy some more petrol.'

'Diesel,' muttered Stanley.

Sparky glanced at him.

'Not petrol, diesel. Buses run on diesel.'

'Do they?' said Sparky. She turned back to the bus driver. 'So perhaps you could buy some of that.'

The driver looked grumpier than ever. 'Are you trying to be funny?' she demanded. 'I've been stuck at roadworks ten times today. I've had fourteen people yell at me for being late. I haven't had any lunch because I forgot to pick up my sandwiches. And I've got back ache fit to make a grizzly bear grizzle. Not only that, it's meant to be my day off but Roland called in sick. So don't you try to be clever or you can get off my bus **right now!**'

Sparky's eyes widened. 'Oh, no, please don't make us get off the bus!' she pleaded. 'I've got to get to the library. I promised I wouldn't be late returning my books and they're due back today. Perhaps you could use our bus fare to buy yourself some more sandwiches. Or you could treat yourself to some chocolate. Mum always says there's no harm in treating yourself now and again.'

The bus driver leaned back in her seat and stared at Sparky. 'Does she really? Well, if I was your mum,' she said, 'I don't think I'd let you out on your own.'

Sparky stared back. 'I'm not on my own,' she replied. 'I'm with Stanley.' She felt a little offended. Never in her life had she come across such a rude bus driver.

The driver's eyes slid towards Stanley who stood, hands in his pockets, trying as hard as he could to look as though he wasn't with anyone.

Once again, Sparky held out the £20 note. 'Anyway, we need to get to the library before it shuts,' she said. 'So may we have two return tickets, please?'

The driver heaved an enormous sigh. 'Now we're back where we started, aren't we? What am I supposed to do with a £20 note? I'm not made of change, am I?'

Sparky pictured the bus driver as a big pile of change. She imagined the heap of coins driving the bus, clinking and chinking every time it turned the steering wheel.

'Oh,' she said. 'Haven't you got any change at all?'

'Yes, of course I've got *some* change,' snapped the driver. 'What kind of a driver would I be if I had no change? But if everyone who got on the bus today gave me a £20 note, my change wouldn't last long, would it?'

'*Has* everyone who got on the bus today given you a £20 note?' Sparky asked.

'No,' said the driver. 'But if they had, imagine the problem I'd have.'

Sparky decided that the driver's main problem was being rude and grumpy. But as Sparky was neither rude nor grumpy (most of the time), she didn't say so. She just smiled and said 'thank you' when the driver finally handed her the change from the £20 note.

'Well, some people!' she whispered to Stanley as she slipped into the seat beside him. 'What a lot of fuss over a little bit of change.'

Stanley stared out of the window, a disgruntled expression on his face. 'Don't talk to me about fuss,' he grumbled. 'I shouldn't even be here, I've got homework to do. I have got a life, you know.'

The journey to the library was **painfully slow**.

'This journey is *painfully* slow,' said Sparky. 'That's what Mum would say. *Painfully* slow.'

Every traffic light turned red just before the bus reached it. There were extra traffic lights too that weren't usually there, because of roadworks. And it was the end of the day so there were queues round every corner. The streets were jammed with cars driven by people trying to get home.

Stanley lost count of the number of times Sparky asked, 'What's the time, please, Stanley?... What time is it now?... Can you tell me the time?'

When Sparky began to moan, 'We're never going to get there in time. The library will close – we just won't get there!' – Stanley replied, 'I could have told you that before we left home.'

As the bus crawled along a particularly slow section of the main road, Sparky stood up and hurried to the front.

'Please,' she said to the driver, 'is there any chance at all you could drive just a little bit faster? The library's going to shut soon, and –'

The driver interrupted. 'If you want to take over and drive the bus instead of me, you're very welcome.'

If only I could, Sparky thought. *I couldn't possibly drive any more slowly than this.*

She sat back down and fidgeted and jiggled her knees up and down. 'We'd be there in no time if this was a flying bus, Stanley,' she said.

Stanley looked at her. 'I think you'll find a flying bus is called an aeroplane.'

The bus ground to a halt yet again.

'Do you suppose God would help if I asked Him, Stanley?' Sparky said. 'After all, I *am* trying to keep a promise. God would want me to keep a promise, wouldn't He?'

'I don't think God's going to make the bus fly, if that's what you mean,' answered Stanley.

Sparky rolled her eyes. 'Obviously I'm not expecting God to make the bus fly,' she said. 'I just want Him to help me not break my promise.'

Sparky found that God was always helpful – which wasn't how she found her brother. Whenever she talked to God about a problem or a worry, she felt better. Even if nothing seemed to change straightaway. Even if a situation didn't turn out as she had hoped. Just talking to God made her feel lighter inside. She knew He was listening.

The bus continued to stop and start, to jolt and rattle, to creak and trundle. Until at last it reached the library.

'What time is it, Stanley?' Sparky asked.

Stanley looked at his watch. Again. 'A minute after half past six. We've missed it. It'll be shut.'

'No, it won't!' Sparky insisted. 'Come on, let's go!'

As the bus came to a halt, she jumped out of her seat and rushed down the aisle. The door folded itself to one side.

Stanley followed more slowly.

'Thank you!' Sparky called to the driver as she hopped off the bus and onto the pavement. She didn't really think she had anything to thank the driver for, but she said it anyway. Grandad always thanked the driver when he got off the bus. But perhaps he'd never been driven by someone quite so rude.

'Yes, well,' said the driver, 'next time you catch the bus, try to have the right change!'

Sparky didn't reply. She'd already run the short distance to the library steps.

'Stanley, come *on*!' she shouted, and she launched herself up the steps to the main door. Once outside the door, however, she couldn't quite bring herself to push on it. If the door was locked, Sparky's promise was broken.

'You open it, Stanley,' Sparky said.

'Why me?' Stanley asked.

'Because if it's locked, I don't want to be the one to find out.'

'But you'll find out it's locked when I push on it and it doesn't open.'

'Oh, just try the door, Stanley, please!'

Stanley shrugged his shoulders. 'All right, I'll try the door. But it's gone half past six. It'll be locked.'

Stanley stepped forward and leaned against the swing door. It opened. Much to Stanley's surprise.

As he wasn't expecting the door to move, he'd leant on it rather more heavily than was sensible. Lurching through the opening, he lost his balance and fell flat on his back.

YOU SEEN THIS EMU?
JUMBLE SALE

'It's open, Stanley!' cried Sparky. Her face beamed with delight. She ignored the fact that her brother was sprawled on the floor and hopped over him. 'I can keep my promise! The library's open!'

Sparky skipped over to the main desk and pulled her books out of her bag. She put them down on the desk top and waited for the librarian, with a huge smile on her face.

Stanley joined her and waited too. A few minutes passed.

'It's very quiet in here,' Stanley said.

'It's always quiet in the library,' said Sparky. 'People come here to be quiet and choose books.'

'I know that,' Stanley replied. 'But I don't think I've ever noticed it this quiet before.'

Another few minutes went by.

'Sparky?' said Stanley. 'All the lights are off.'

Sparky glanced around. In her excitement, this was something she hadn't noticed. But now that Stanley mentioned it, she realised that the inside of the library was rather dim.

'Well, it is almost closing time,' she said. 'The librarian's probably turned the lights off ready to go home.'

'But where *is* the librarian?' Stanley asked.

'I don't know. Upstairs maybe? I'll go and see.'

'I'll come with you,' said Stanley.

'No.' Sparky shook her head. 'You stay here in case she shows up at the desk.'

'But...' Stanley looked uncertain. 'I think I should go with you. Mum wouldn't want me to let you go on your own.'

Sparky frowned. 'We're in the library, Stanley. What could possibly happen to me in the library?'

'I don't know.' Stanley shrugged his shoulders. 'I just think we should stick together, that's all.'

'Are you scared to be left here by yourself?' Sparky's eyes narrowed.

'No!' Stanley replied quickly. 'Of course I'm not scared! Who gets scared in a library? Not me.'

'Right,' said Sparky. 'Then you stay here and look out for the librarian and I'll go upstairs in case she's there.'

'I'm coming with you,' Stanley said. 'I'm not scared. But it's dark and creepy in here, and I'm not letting you wander off on your own. That's all.'

Sparky peered at him. 'You *are* scared, aren't you?' The corners of her mouth twitched as she tried not to giggle.

'I'm not scared!' Stanley repeated. 'I'm coming with you to make sure *you* don't get scared.'

'Oh, I *see*!' said Sparky. She stopped trying not to giggle and giggled her way towards the stairs. 'Come on, then – **scaredy cat**.'

Just like downstairs, there were no lights on upstairs in the library. Nor was there any sign of anyone, let alone a librarian. The silence was deafening.

'The silence up here is deafening,' said Stanley. 'That's what Mum would say. The silence is *deafening*.'

'Hello?' Sparky called into the dimness.

No answer.

She tried again. 'Is there anyone here? I've come to bring back my books.'

Silence.

Stanley looked around uneasily. 'I think we should go back downstairs.'

'I'll just go to the end,' said Sparky. 'There might be an office or something.'

'I'll come with you,' Stanley said, 'so you don't get scared.'

'Of course,' replied Sparky. 'So *I* don't get scared.'

They didn't find an office because there wasn't one. But Sparky did spot several books on how to crochet.

'Oh, look, Stanley!' she cried. 'Crochet books. I should get these out for Grandad. He'd love them. Oh, and look!' Sparky's eye had fallen on another book. 'This one tells you how to make your home smell nice.'

She pulled it out and flicked through the pages. 'I think I'll get this one out for Mum. Maybe there'll be some useful tips so our house doesn't have to smell like Dad's sweaty personal training kit ever again.'

'Is there a book on how to not forget to return your library books?' asked Stanley.

'I don't think so,' said Sparky.

'Then I really don't think you should get any more books out for now, do you?'

Sparky and Stanley made their way back to the staircase. Sparky called out, 'Hello?' a couple of times on the way and, 'Are there any librarians up here?'

No librarians answered.

There still wasn't a librarian at the main desk downstairs either.

'I think we should just leave your books and go,' said Stanley.

'But someone has to check them back in,' said Sparky. 'Otherwise I might still get a fine.'

'No, you won't,' replied Stanley. 'You've brought your

books back. That's all you have to do.'

'I know,' Sparky said, 'I'll leave a note.'

There was a pot of pens on the desk top but no paper.

'Stanley, do you have any paper?' Sparky asked.

Stanley blinked at her. 'Why would I have paper?'

'I don't know, but I need to leave a note.'

'You don't need to leave a note, Sparky. You're leaving the books.'

Sparky was about to slip behind the desk to look for paper when one of her brilliant ideas popped into her head.

'The toilets!' she said, as her eyes sparkled. 'Toilets are full of paper.'

'Sparky,' Stanley began, 'no one's going to want a note written on toilet paper –'

Too late. Sparky had already darted into the toilets by the main door. She reappeared moments later with a square of tissue.

'Dear Invisible Librarian Person,' she wrote. 'Here are my books. They are due back today so I've kept my promise. Lots of love, Sparky Smart.'

When she'd finished writing, she placed the piece of tissue on top of the pile of books.

'Hmm...' she said. 'Tissue is very light. My note might blow away.'

'Good point,' said Stanley. 'Because libraries are well known for being windy. Can we just leave now, please?'

Sparky sighed. 'I suppose so,' she replied. 'Goodbye, Invisible Librarian Person.' And with that, she followed Stanley towards the door.

Stanley put out a hand to pull one of the swing

doors open.

It didn't move.

Weird, Stanley thought. *I'm sure that's the door I fell through.*

Without thinking too much of it, he pulled on the other door.

That one didn't move either. Things were getting weirder and weirder.

'You're not pulling hard enough, Stanley,' said Sparky. 'I'll do it.'

Sparky pulled hard on one door and then on the other. Neither would budge.

'They must be stuck,' said Stanley. 'That's what it is – they're stuck.' He yanked on both handles together. Still the doors wouldn't move, so he gave them a sharp shake. They rattled but stayed shut.

Sparky said, 'Let's both try,' and together they grasped the handles and shook the doors.

Stanley's face turned a little pale as he realised why the doors wouldn't open. 'They're locked,' he said.

'They can't be locked,' answered Sparky. 'We wouldn't have got in if they were locked.'

'Well, they're definitely locked now.' Stanley gave the doors another hard shake to prove it. 'I don't believe it, Sparky. I've got homework to do – and we're locked in the library!'

Sparky shook her head. 'No, we're not. We can't be. There must be another door. I expect the librarians lock this door so that no one can get in after they've closed. But then they let the people who are already in here out through another door.'

Stanley looked around. 'I don't see another door,' he said.

Sparky couldn't see another door either. 'It's probably round the back. Let's go and find the librarian and she can show us.'

Stanley stared at her. 'Sparky, we've been looking for the librarian ever since we got here. There isn't a librarian!'

'There must be. Who else would have locked the door?' Sparky argued. 'Hello?' she called. 'Hello, is anyone here?'

But no one was.

Eventually, they did spot another door round the corner behind the staircase. Sparky tried it but it was locked like the swing doors at the front. There was a third door near the little café too, but guess what? It wouldn't open.

'This is impossible, Stanley,' Sparky said. 'You know that, don't you? It's not possible that all the doors are locked, when there were doors open to let us in when we got here. We are *impossibly* locked in the library.'

'I know!' Stanley's face was a mixture of gloom and crossness. 'And I hope *you* know that it's all your fault!'

Sparky's mouth fell open. 'It's *not* my fault! *I* didn't lock the doors. All I've been trying to do is keep a promise.'

'It *is* your fault! If it wasn't for you making a stupid promise about your stupid library books, I wouldn't even be here!'

Sparky sucked in a breath to shout back, but stopped herself.

I know what this is, she thought. *This is Stanley getting in a panic*. Sparky knew there was no point in panicking. Panic never got anyone anywhere.

'There's no point in panicking, Stanley,' she said. 'Panic never got anyone anywhere. That's what Grandad would say, isn't it?' She tried to make her voice sound soothing, like Grandad's would be if he were locked in the library with them.

Grandad's soothing voice was exactly how Sparky imagined God's voice to be. Quiet and calm and kind. She imagined God's face to be calm and kind too. However anxious she was, however sad or worried, God was always ready to take her hand and say, 'Panic never got anyone anywhere. It'll all be fine. I'm right here with you.'

Sparky was sure that knowing God was with them in the library was why she wasn't in a panic herself.

'Besides, Stanley,' she went on, 'we're not stuck. All we've got to do is phone Mum and Dad and they'll come and let us out.'

Stanley scowled. 'How? Mum and Dad don't have a key to the library.'

'Well, we'll phone them anyway. They're bound to know what to do.'

'And what if they don't?'

'If they don't...' Sparky considered this for a moment. 'If they don't, what's the worst that can happen? We'll have to spend the night in the library, that's all.'

Stanley's eyes looked as though they might pop out of his head. 'But I don't want to spend the night in the library!'

'Stanley, it's one night. The librarian will be back in the morning. As soon as she unlocks the door, we can go home for breakfast.'

'I'm supposed to be at home *now*, doing my homework,' moaned Stanley. 'I have got a life, you know.'

'I think it's actually rather exciting,' said Sparky. '**We're locked in the library!** That's never happened to us before – ever. And to think not long ago this was just a normal day!'

Stanley flopped down onto the floor and sat with his back against the main doors. He didn't look as though he thought it was exciting at all. Stanley liked normal.

'Go on, then,' said Sparky. 'Ring home.'

Stanley started to feel around in his pockets for his

phone. 'You can be the one to tell Mum,' he grumbled. 'She's going to be hopping mad... Oh...'

'What?' Sparky looked at him. Stanley seemed to have stopped searching his pockets.

'I haven't got my phone,' he mumbled.

'You must have. Mum told you to bring it because she didn't want us out and about on our own without a phone.'

'I know,' Stanley grunted.

'It's the last thing she said before we got the bus.'

'I *know*.'

'So why haven't you got it?'

Stanley dropped his head and began to gnaw at his thumbnail. 'I didn't pick it up,' he mumbled at last.

'Why not?'

'Because we were only going to the library. Why would I need my phone when we were *only* going to the library?'

Sparky threw her hands up in the air. (She'd seen Mrs Smart do this many times when things weren't going to plan. She quite enjoyed this opportunity to do it herself.) Everyone else Stanley's age seemed to never let their phone out of their sight. Yet here *he* was, without his phone when they *really* needed it.

'But we do need it, don't we, Stanley? I know it's not normal to get locked in a library but it's obviously something that can happen – because it has! And when you're locked in a library, what you really need is a phone. And that's not the only reason why you should have brought it. You should have brought it because Mum told you to!'

Stanley glared. 'Well, you should have taken your

library books back on time and not left it until the last minute, but that didn't happen either!'

There was silence. For a moment, even Sparky's quick-thinking brain went quiet. Then it sprang back into action.

'It doesn't matter anyway,' she said. She pointed behind her to the main desk. 'This is a library. *They've* got a phone.'

Instantly Sparky marched to the desk. She picked up the phone, dialled their home number and waited for the ring tone.

'Mum'll have us out before we know it, you'll see,' she said to Stanley as she waited... and waited...

Not a sound came from the phone. Even when she pressed it harder to her ear, there wasn't a peep (or rather a ring).

She hung up and tried again, jabbing the number keys down harder this time.

'That's really weird,' she said. 'Shouldn't there be a buzzy noise before you dial?' She shook the handset and listened again. 'Because there isn't. I don't think this phone's working.'

'Of course it's working,' said Stanley. 'This is the library. It has to have a working phone.' He heaved himself to his feet. 'You're obviously not doing it right. Give it to me.'

Stanley was about to dial when his eyebrows inched together in a frown. He put the phone down heavily onto its cradle, lifted it up and put it to his ear again. He did the same thing twice more. Then he looked at Sparky and gave his head a dismal shake.

'This phone's not working,' he said.

Sparky blinked. 'I know it's not working. *I* told *you* that.'

'This phone's dead,' Stanley went on, as if she hadn't spoken. 'There's no dialling tone, nothing. We're locked in the library with a dead phone and no way out.' He put the phone down and stared at it hopelessly. 'You know what this means, don't you?'

'No, Stanley, what does it mean?' Sparky listened expectantly.

'It means this is it for us. We're cut off from the outside world.'

'No, we're not!' Sparky scoffed.

'We are, though,' Stanley insisted. '**Cut off... locked away... doomed...**'

Sparky gazed at her brother. It occurred to her that however tricky a situation might seem, Stanley always made it seem trickier.

'We're not doomed, Stanley,' she said. 'For one thing, Mum knows where we are. When we don't come home, she'll know exactly where to come looking.'

Stanley slumped to the floor and leaned against the wooden front of the main desk. 'I suppose this is what it's like to be shipwrecked. Washed up all alone on a desert island.' His voice was filled with gloom. 'We can't let anyone know where we are. We can't call for help. We're stranded. All we can do is wait and hope that someone will find us. It could be hours. Days. Even weeks...'

He sat forward suddenly and pulled his right foot towards him. 'And on top of that, I've got a really sore toe. I think my blister must have popped.'

Sparky raised an eyebrow. 'I didn't know you had a blister.'

Stanley slid his right foot out of its shoe and carefully

peeled off his sock. He turned his foot upside down and peered at his big toe.

'Well, I have,' Stanley groaned. 'Only now, it's a popped blister and they're the worst kind. See?'

He thrust his foot towards Sparky. She squealed and backed away.

'**Ugh!**' Stanley grunted. 'Could this day get any worse?!'

Sparky would have loved to point out the obvious: that if Stanley had brought his phone like Mrs Smart had told him to, they wouldn't be cut off, doomed, shipwrecked, stranded or anything else. But she didn't want to start an argument. After all, she was the one who'd forgotten about her library books and Stanley had very kindly gone with her to the library on the bus. Without him, her promise would have been broken.

Not only that, but Grandad had told them lots of times that nothing was worth arguing over.

'Most of the time I'd bite my tongue rather than start an argument,' he'd say.

Sparky had always found the idea of biting your tongue so that you don't argue quite strange. But as she held her tongue between her teeth in an effort not to remind Stanley about his mobile phone, she realised how clever Grandad was. With her tongue trapped, it was just about impossible to say anything at all, let alone anything that anyone would be able to understand. (Try it the next time you think you might say something you shouldn't. But don't bite too hard, of course, because that would be silly.)

Sparky sat on the floor next to her brother. (But not

until he'd put his sock and shoe back on. Never in a million years would she sit next to a bare popped blister.)

'I think we should ask God what to do,' she said. 'He's not just for church on Sundays, Stanley. Mum says that, doesn't she? When we walk out of the door at the end of the service, we don't leave Him behind. He comes with us. He's for every day of the week, every week of the year and everywhere we go. And He'll especially be in a locked-up library.'

Stanley shook his head. 'God probably just thinks I'm stupid for leaving my phone at home.'

'He doesn't. God doesn't think anyone's stupid.' She paused, then added, 'Anyway you're right. This *is* all my fault because I forgot about my library books. But I don't think God thinks I'm stupid either.'

Stanley stared at his hurting foot. Sparky wasn't sure if he was thinking about God or his blister.

'Tell you what,' she said after a moment or two, 'I'll talk to God for both of us.'

In the quiet of the empty library, Sparky prayed.

'Dear God, when I woke up this morning, I thought it was going to be a normal day. There were a few things that weren't *quite* normal, but that's what made it so normal. Only now it's not a normal day at all. There can't be many people who take their books back to the library and end up getting locked in. In fact, this is probably the first time it's ever happened. And I'm sorry I forgot about my books, and Stanley's sorry he didn't pick up his phone. But if You could please help us know what to do, that would be very kind. Thank You.'

'I wish the café was open,' Stanley said. 'I'm starving.'

Now that Stanley mentioned it, Sparky realised she was starving too.

'I wonder how long it'll be before Mum notices we haven't come home,' she said. 'She's bound to realise sooner or later.'

'And when she does, you know what she'll do, don't you? She'll ring my phone. Which she'll hear ringing in my bedroom. Which means I'll be in trouble for the rest of my life.'

'Not the rest of your life, Stanley.' Sparky gave him an encouraging smile. 'Only the rest of the year.'

As Stanley continued to stare at his foot and Sparky gazed at the library's main doors, suddenly, the answer to their difficulties leapt out and hit her right between the eyes. (It didn't *actually* hit her between the eyes, obviously. That would have hurt and probably been quite dangerous. It's just an expression.)

'*I* know!' she cried. In just a second, she'd jumped to her feet. 'Why didn't I think of it before? I know exactly how to get out of here!'

Stanley looked doubtful. He didn't jump anywhere.

'It's as simple as anything, Stanley!' Sparky went on. 'We'll bang on the doors! We'll bang really hard and we'll shout for help. And when everyone turns to look at where the noise is coming from, they'll see us behind the glass and have us out in no time!'

Stanley still didn't move. 'When you say "everyone",' he said, 'not a lot of people walk along here unless they want to go to the library. It's not like there's shops or anything. And they won't want to go to the library now because they'll know it's shut.'

'But some people will,' Sparky insisted. 'Next time a bus stops, people will get off. In fact' – her eyes shone with her own inventiveness – 'there might be people waiting at the bus stop right now!'

She charged across the wide hall to the main door. In her mind she could see a whole queue of people standing in a line at the bus shelter. A whole queue of helpful, smiling, happy people just waiting to rescue them!

Little did they know, she thought, that they were all about to become superheroes for setting free the children locked in the library! They'd be interviewed on the TV news... They'd have their pictures in the local paper... They'd...

Sparky peered through the glass in the door. 'Oh...'

There was no sign of anyone. And the picture of the queue of superheroes inside her head vanished.

'Told you,' grunted Stanley.

Never one to be beaten, Sparky said, 'I don't care. I'm going to bang on the door anyway. Because you never know who may come running. That's what Grandad would say in this situation. "You never know..."'

Stanley made a face. 'How do you know what Grandad would say in this situation? When has Grandad ever been locked in a library?'

With her hands screwed into fists, Sparky began to bang hard on the glass doors. 'Help!' she yelled at nobody because there was nobody there to yell at. 'Help! We're locked in the library! You've got to get us out! Help! *Heeelllppp*!!'

No one appeared. No one came running.

'See?' Stanley muttered. 'Waste of time.'

'It's not a waste of time, Stanley,' Sparky replied. 'All we need is one person... one tiny little person...'

She continued to thump and shout.

At long last, after much banging and screaming, when Sparky's hands had started to hurt and her throat had gone dry and scratchy, two people did appear. A man and a woman, who weren't tiny but were a normal sort of size. They scurried along in the pouring rain, huddled under a large, black umbrella.

As soon as Sparky spotted them, she began to bang even harder and yell even louder.

To her amazement, the two people took almost no notice at all. The man did seem to hesitate at one point and turn his head towards the library. But the woman just pulled him along after her until they were out of sight.

Sparky's sore hands dropped to her sides. 'Well, that's just mean!' she croaked. 'How could they not have heard me? And if they did hear me, how could they not come and help?'

She stared out into the rainy evening. She looked up and down the pavement that was all wet and empty for as far as she could see. She gazed towards the empty bus stop.

Inside her head a voice said, 'Stanley's right. You're doomed.' But she pressed her lips hard together and refused to listen to it. She certainly wasn't going to let Stanley hear it.

It was while her lips were still pressed hard together that someone else appeared.

Has something ever happened to you where you've

thought, if I tell anyone about this, they'll never believe it? Well, the thing that was about to happen to Sparky and Stanley was exactly one of those things.

A woman walked round the corner. She was tall and thin, dressed in a long, sensible-looking raincoat buttoned up to her chin. And she wasn't scurrying like the man and woman, she walked quite slowly; the same sort of speed she would have walked in either the rain or the sun, Sparky imagined. Her umbrella wasn't as big as the man and woman's either, nor was it black. This umbrella was red with a pattern of white cats scampering across it.

It was an umbrella Sparky was sure she'd seen somewhere before...

'Miss Clatworthy...' Sparky murmured. Then, more loudly: '**Miss Clatworthy!**'

'What?' Stanley looked up. He'd taken his shoe off again and was inspecting his blister.

'Miss Clatworthy! Stanley, it's Miss Clatworthy!' Sparky squealed. 'Come and help – *now*!'

As Sparky began to thump and thud on the doors again with her poor, sore fists, Stanley leapt up and raced across the hallway to join her – at least, he hopped very quickly, his one bare, blistered foot dangling in mid-air. Together, they pounded on the library doors and screamed and shouted at the tops of their voices:

'Miss Clatworthy, help! Help us, please! Miss Clatworthy, it's us – *heeelllppp*!!'

Miss Clatworthy, who lived next door to the Smarts on Priory Park, wasn't used to being yelled at by anyone anywhere. (Although she used to be a head teacher, so it's quite possible that she herself had done a fair amount of yelling in the past.)

Generally, if she heard anyone yell, she made it her business to ignore them.

'If anyone yells,' Miss Clatworthy told her cats, Monday, Tuesday and Thursday, 'look the other way. People who yell definitely aren't the sort of people we want to have anything to do with.'

However, as Sparky and Stanley's yelling reached her ears, Miss Clatworthy felt she had to stop.

This wasn't just any old yelling. This yelling was an urgent kind of yelling. It was muffled and distant, the sort of yelling that meant something wasn't right.

The sort of yelling, in fact, that told her something was very, very wrong.

Not only that, but in the midst of one yell after the other, Miss Clatworthy was sure she heard her name...

'Miss Clatworthy – **HEEELLLPPP!!**'

Sparky and Stanley had been thumping on the doors and shouting their hearts out. When they saw Miss Clatworthy hesitate on the pavement, they thumped and shouted even louder.

Moving her head, Miss Clatworthy tried to work out where the shouting was coming from. The noise from cars and vans passing by on the road made it harder to work out.

In the hope of attracting her attention to the library, between thumping and yelling, Sparky was now jumping up and down and waving her arms.

Miss Clatworthy began to turn. As she did so, she

looked all around.

When she had almost turned a full circle, her eyes at last came to rest on the library building.

This was it! This was their chance! Sparky leapt up and down as fast as she could. She waved her arms so wildly that one of her flying hands accidentally hit Stanley on the nose. (Luckily, Stanley wasn't wearing his glasses.)

Miss Clatworthy peered through the rain. What was that, moving behind the library doors, bouncing up and down like a mad thing? And why was anything bouncing up and down in the library? Surely the librarian must have gone home by now. Even if she hadn't, why would she be bouncing?

Miss Clatworthy took a few steps forward and peered harder. She was relieved to see that the bouncing thing wasn't the librarian. It looked like... a small child – and next to the child, still thumping and yelling, was someone else. Someone taller.

'In fact,' murmured Miss Clatworthy to herself as she moved closer still, 'if I didn't know better, I'd say that was Stanley and Sabrina Smart...'

'Miss Clatworthy!' Another yell rang out through the locked glass doors of the library. 'It's us, Stanley and Sparky! We're trapped! Please help us! *Please*!'

Miss Clatworthy wasn't exactly the sort of superhero Sparky had imagined when she'd pictured the queue of helpful, smiling, happy people at the bus stop. The idea that their next-door neighbour could be any kind of superhero had never crossed her mind.

As far as Sparky could make out, Miss Clatworthy

didn't like people. She most certainly didn't like children (which was odd given that she'd chosen to be a head teacher). No, all Miss Clatworthy really liked was cats.

So, the fact that it was Miss Clatworthy about to rescue Sparky and Stanley meant that Sparky would probably never be able to look at her in the same light again. From now on, Miss Clatworthy would no longer be the Smarts' cold, unfriendly, disapproving, child-hating neighbour – she'd be a hero. A tall, thin, sensible-raincoat-wearing, buttoned-up hero with a cat umbrella, but a hero nonetheless.

Much as she'd rather have ignored the cries for help and continued on her way to the bus stop, Miss Clatworthy climbed the library steps.

Puffing and panting, with sore fists and scratchy throats (and a bit of a bruised nose in Stanley's case), the two Smarts gazed at her.

'What on earth do you think you're up to?' Miss Clatworthy demanded. She didn't look happy. She never looked happy.

Sparky gulped down some air. 'We're so sorry to bother you,' she croaked. 'And we wouldn't bother you unless it was an absolute emergency.'

Miss Clatworthy glared.

'The thing is...' Sparky began, 'what's happened is... Well, it's not our fault, it's just...'

'We're locked in the library!' Stanley blurted out. 'We came to bring Sparky's books back and someone locked us in. And I've got homework to do. I have got a life, you know.'

Miss Clatworthy continued to glare. 'What do you

mean someone locked you in? *Who* locked you in?'

'We don't know,' Sparky croaked. 'We think it was probably the librarian, but we don't know why. We couldn't find her.'

Miss Clatworthy was a surprising person in many ways, Sparky decided. Not only did she have a mobile phone – Sparky never imagined someone like Miss Clatworthy would even want a mobile phone – but she also just happened to be friends with the librarian. Apparently, the librarian had three cats too, and she and Miss Clatworthy went out sometimes for tea and cake.

Whether they talked about cats or books didn't matter. What did matter was that Miss Clatworthy had the librarian's number stored in her phone and was able to ring her up and sort out the whole mess. Just like that.

Apparently, the librarian had closed the library, set the burglar alarm and locked the doors as usual at closing time. However, as she'd trotted down the steps, she'd realised her umbrella wasn't in her bag. So, she'd run back up again, unlocked the doors, turned off the burglar alarm and popped behind the desk to fetch it.

The umbrella wasn't there. That's when she remembered she'd left it in the staff cloakroom, and off she went to find it.

While in the cloakroom, the librarian happened to glance in the mirror and she noticed a small splash of something on the collar of her raincoat. So she dampened the corner of her hankie under the tap and tried to rub it off. It wouldn't budge, not even when she used soap.

It was while she was in the cloakroom, rubbing at her

collar and wondering how much it would cost to get her raincoat properly cleaned, that Stanley and Sparky had walked through the unlocked doors and into the library.

As the librarian had sighed and tutted and fretted about her favourite coat, Stanley and Sparky had waited at the desk to give her Sparky's books.

But she hadn't appeared. So Sparky and Stanley had gone to look for her upstairs.

While they were up there, the librarian had realised there was nothing more she could do for her coat in the cloakroom. So, she'd picked up her umbrella and, having no idea there was anyone inside, had left the building, locking the doors behind her.

What she'd forgotten to do was turn on the burglar alarm again. If she had, Sparky and Stanley would have set it off and someone would have come to investigate. But the librarian was so flustered by the mysterious stain on her collar that it had gone right out of her head.

When Sparky and Stanley came back downstairs, they found no librarian – and no way out of the library.

It was as simple as that.

(The phone, by the way, was working, but you had to press the number '5' button to get the buzzy sound.)

* * * *

Sparky and Stanley sat together on the sofa in their house at Priory Park. They sipped steaming mugs of hot chocolate.

'It's been an interesting day, hasn't it, Stanley?' Sparky said. 'Not normal at all, as it turns out.'

‘Really?’ Stanley replied. ‘Getting locked in a library isn’t what I’d call interesting.’

‘But it was, though,’ Sparky went on. ‘Think about it. There’s *so* much more to Miss Clatworthy than we ever realised. I’ll never say anything mean about her ever again.’

‘Huh,’ grunted Stanley.

‘And Mum wasn’t *that* cross with you for leaving your phone behind. And you’ve actually learnt a really good lesson.’

‘Have I?’

‘Yes. You now know how important it is to do as Mum says and take your phone when we go out on our own together.’

‘Pah!’ scoffed Stanley. ‘It doesn’t matter now because I’m never going out with you on my own ever again.’

‘And on top of all that,’ Sparky continued, ‘we know what it’s like to be all alone, locked in a library – which I think is very interesting indeed.’

‘Ugh!’ huffed Stanley.

‘But, do you know what the most interesting thing about today is?’ Sparky asked. ‘We didn’t argue. There we were, **shipwrecked at the library**, marooned and doomed, and we didn’t argue once. Not really. We helped each other. Even though you were grumpy and scared to be left downstairs on your own, we still helped each other.’

‘I wasn’t scared,’ said Stanley.

‘Well, all right, but we both helped each other, didn’t we, Stanley?’ said Sparky. ‘And do you know what that means?’

‘No.’

Sparky put down her hot chocolate and swivelled on the sofa to face him. 'We did it God's way. We had a problem and we sorted it out God's way.'

Stanley looked at her. 'Did we?'

'Yes,' said Sparky. 'One hundred per cent. That's what Dad would say, isn't it? *God's way. One hundred per cent.*'

Zoo hullabaloo

'I've told you a hundred times – there's no need for you to drive us to the station, Stella. There's no need for you to drive us anywhere. I'll do it.'

Auntie Bella pushed and shoved and tried with all her strength to ram Sparky's coat into a canvas bag that was large, but not large enough. The bag already bulged with snacks, water bottles, three coats belonging to herself and her twins (Nat and Archie) and a picnic blanket.

Sparky's coat just wasn't going to fit, no matter how much Auntie Bella wanted it to.

'Do you want some help?' asked Mrs Smart. Mrs Smart

was Auntie Bella's twin sister. 'Mind you, I'm not sure that bag's big enough.'

'**No!**' snapped Auntie Bella. 'I don't need any help. Honestly, Stella, you're always on about how you never get a break. Well, look at me – I'm trying to give you a break right now. Stanley's off with a friend. I'm taking Sparky off your hands. You can spend the rest of the day with your feet up, munching your way through a packet of Jammie Dodgers if you want to.'

'Erm... not quite,' said Mrs Smart.

Auntie Bella looked put out and tried again to shove Sparky's coat into the bag. 'Why ever not? You do like to make things difficult for yourself, don't you?'

'Well... I have still got Sissy.'

'Who?'

Mrs Smart stood in the kitchen doorway, her youngest child, Sissy, clasped to her hip.

Auntie Bella paused and glanced up. 'Oh, of course, what's-her-name.' She tutted. 'Well, if you will insist on having three children, Stell. Two's what I wanted and two's what I've got and that's more than enough, if you want my opinion.' (Mrs Smart didn't.) 'Then you'll just have to share your Jammie Dodgers with little... thingy... won't you?'

Auntie Bella made one last attempt with Sparky's coat. 'But at least you'll have a day with only one child to worry about. *I'll* be the one with three to cart around instead!'

Realising that the battle of the coat wasn't going to be won, Auntie Bella at last gave up and threw it on the hall floor. 'Not even bags are designed for three children,' she grumbled.

'I can just carry my coat,' said Sparky. She stepped forward to pick it up.

'I do have a bigger bag,' added Mrs Smart.

'I don't want a bigger bag,' Auntie Bella replied, her mood getting worse by the second. 'This one's enough of a pain to lug around as it is.'

There was silence for a moment. Then Mrs Smart said, 'Bella, do you really *want* to take the children to the zoo?'

'Of course I want to take them. I loved it last time I went.'

'Last time you went, you were probably only a child yourself.' Mrs Smart looked anxious, though she was trying hard not to. She wasn't happy with the whole idea. In fact, she'd spent at least two hours of the previous night lying awake worrying about it.

The worrying had made no difference. This was a situation she seemed to be stuck with.

The evening before had gone like this...

'Mum, phone's ringing! Shall I answer it?' Sparky ran into the kitchen to find Mrs Smart.

Just at that moment, Mrs Smart didn't care about the ringing phone. She didn't care who was on the other end or what they wanted either. She was too busy trying to unblock the kitchen sink with a plunger.

If you've never tried to unblock a sink with a plunger, you may not know just how much of an effort it can be. And it's not the sort of task where you want interruptions. Especially when the blockage is sizable – which this one was.

The blockage had come about partly because Mrs Smart had just made a cake and partly because she'd left the kitchen to answer a different phone call.

'I'll be two minutes,' she'd said to Sissy. 'Wait there.'

As often happened when Mrs Smart answered the phone, she was longer than two minutes. While she'd chatted away, little Sissy had decided to help herself to the half bag of flour that Mrs Smart had rather unwisely left out on the table.

Sissy had taken the flour, sprinkled some on the floor and run around, making footprints (with and without socks on). She'd then pushed a chair to the kitchen sink, climbed onto it and poured the rest of the flour – the rest being quite a lot – into the sink itself.

The situation might not have been so bad if she hadn't then turned on the taps. But for Sissy, the chance to mix up flour and water was just too exciting. It was such fun to squidge her fingers into the stodgy, sticky, gooey heap.

It was even more fun to squish it down the plughole...

By the time Mrs Smart had got off the phone, the sink was completely blocked. So when the phone rang again, she was far too busy with the plunger to bother with it.

'Don't worry,' Sparky had said, 'I'll get it... Hello, Sparky Smart speaking. How may I help you?'

Sparky had heard people in shops answer phones like this. (Not with the name 'Sparky Smart', obviously, but with their own names.) She thought it sounded kind and clever so had decided this was how she would answer the phone in future too.

'Hello, Sparky, it's Auntie Bella,' came the voice on the other end. 'Is your mum there?'

Sparky had peered round the kitchen door. Mrs Smart was still busy plunging. A lot of strange gurgling could be heard.

'Well...' Sparky replied, 'she is and she isn't. What I mean is, she is, because she's in the kitchen. But she isn't, because she can't come to the phone.'

'Never mind. It's really you I want to talk to anyway.'

'Is it?' said Sparky. She felt pleased. It wasn't often a grown-up rang the Smarts and wanted to talk to Sparky. Perhaps she'd won Auntie Bella over with her new telephone-answering phrase.

'Would you like to come to the zoo with us tomorrow?' Auntie Bella asked. 'I'm taking Nat and Archie so I thought you could tag along. I'd take Stanley too, but I don't think he'll fit in the car.'

Sparky's eyebrows shot up. This was a very unusual phone call. Usually when Auntie Bella rang it was to ask Mrs Smart if *she* would take Nat and Archie off her hands or have them to stay for a few days. The last thing Sparky expected was for it to be the other way round.

Auntie Bella never invited Stanley or Sparky anywhere. She had *more* than enough to cope with, she said (a lot): 'I'm bringing up my boys on my own and I have a very busy job writing articles for a magazine. Please don't ask me to cram anything else in or I'll have a nervous breakdown!'

'Stanley's not here tomorrow,' Sparky began – he was going to his friend's house for the day – 'but I'd *love* to go! I've never been to the zoo before.'

'I have,' Auntie Bella replied. 'Years ago but I remember it being rather fun – all animals and things, you know. There was a shop, too, I think. I remember liking the shop.'

'I'll just check with Mum but I'm sure she'll say I can go,' Sparky said.

'No, don't bother. You want to go, that's good enough. Just tell her I'll pick you up at nine o'clock tomorrow morning. We'll drive to the station and go on the train.'

'The train?!' Sparky's eyes gleamed. She loved going on the train.

'Yes, the train. If I try to drive to the zoo, I'll never find it. See you in the morning then. Now at least your mum can't say she never gets a break – she'll have the whole of tomorrow off, with no children to look after.'

'Apart from Sissy,' Sparky reminded her.

'Who?' Auntie Bella said. 'Oh, never mind. Byeee!'

And she was gone.

'Mum!' Sparky had charged into the kitchen. 'Auntie Bella's taking me, Nat and Archie to the zoo tomorrow.'

Mrs Smart was hot and red in the face from all the plunging. 'It's no good,' she said, 'It's blocked solid. I think I'm going to have to get a plumber in.'

'And we're going on the train,' squealed Sparky. 'Isn't that so cool?'

'Mind you,' Mrs Smart continued, 'I don't know how quickly I'll be able to get a plumber to come out.'

'She's coming at nine o'clock in the morning and we're driving to the station.'

'I wish your dad was a bit handier with a spanner. I don't know how long I can manage without a working sink.'

'We have to go on the train,' said Sparky. 'Auntie Bella says she won't find it if she has to drive.'

'Oh, I don't know, perhaps there'll be something Dad can do.' Mrs Smart hadn't listened to a word. 'I'll have to get him to have a look when he gets in.'

'I'm so excited! I'm going up to tell Stanley.' Sparky skipped to the kitchen door. 'I'm going on the train to the zoo!'

'At least your dad should be home soon. I hope he can remember where he keeps his spanners. No idea when he last used them. I expect they're in the...'

Mrs Smart stopped suddenly. She stared at the kitchen doorway. Sparky had disappeared through it and was halfway up the stairs.

'Wait...' Mrs Smart looked confused. 'Just a minute, Sparky! I'm sorry – you're going on the what to the where? When...?'

And so it was that the following morning, Auntie Bella was about to whisk Sparky off for the day.

Sparky climbed into the back of the car and Mrs Smart leaned in at the open window. This wasn't entirely comfortable with Sissy still hugged to her hip.

'Now, remember what we talked about at breakfast, Sparky,' said Mrs Smart. 'You don't go wandering off on your own. You stay with Auntie Bella and Nat and Archie at all times. Is that clear?'

What Mrs Smart had actually said at breakfast was: 'I can't trust Auntie Bella to keep an eye on *you* so it's up to you to make sure you don't lose sight of *her*. *You're* going to have to be the grown-up today, Sparky, otherwise who knows what'll happen?'

But, of course, Mrs Smart didn't say this in front of Auntie Bella.

'Ooh, you do worry, Stell!' said Auntie Bella. 'We're going to the zoo not the other side of the world. And even if we were going to the other side of the world, there'd be nothing to worry about. Sparky'll be fine, won't you, Sparky?'

The thought of Auntie Bella being in charge of Sparky on the other side of the world was almost too much for Mrs Smart. But it did somehow make the idea of the trip to the zoo a little easier.

'Ring me when you get there, Bella,' Mrs Smart said as Auntie Bella started up the car.

'OK, if I remember – but I probably won't,' Auntie Bella replied. 'You know what I'm like.'

Sadly, Mrs Smart did.

'Off we go then – see you later! Byee!'

'Bye, Sparky!' Mrs Smart called. She just managed to pull her head back from the open window as Auntie Bella revved the engine and zoomed out of the driveway.

'Bye, Mum!' Sparky called back. She twisted in her seat and waved through the back window.

Mrs Smart and Sissy waved too.

'The thing is, Mum,' Sparky had said at breakfast, 'everything will be fine. I know Auntie Bella can be a bit batty but she'd never let anything happen to me.'

'Wouldn't she?' Mrs Smart had looked doubtful.

'Of course not,' Sparky had said. 'Just remember the God part of her.'

'The God part?'

'Yes, the God part. Auntie Bella may not be properly friends with God yet but she still has a God part. God made all of us to be like Him. I've read it in the Bible.'

Mrs Smart blinked at Sparky. It had never actually occurred to her that Auntie Bella might have a God part. But Sparky was right. God *had* created people to be like Him.

Of course, people had got into a muddle when they

began to do things wrong and stopped being God's friends. And because of that, it was as if the God part was hidden. But by making friends with God again, it could be uncovered, polished up and given pride of place – just as it should be.

Sparky was sure that one day, Auntie Bella would have a shiny new life with God right in the middle of it. She prayed for her every day.

Mrs Smart prayed for Auntie Bella too. And from that day forward, when she prayed, she made up her mind to try to remember the God part that was just waiting to be uncovered.

If only it was uncovered already, Mrs Smart had thought. As much as she wanted to trust her sister, with Auntie Bella nothing ever seemed to go to plan...

✲ ✲ ✲ ✲

'Can I sit by the window? *Please?*' asked Sparky.

She stood just inside the carriage and felt she might explode with excitement.

'But *I* like sitting by the window,' said Archie.

'So do I,' said Nat.

Auntie Bella sighed. 'I hate trains.'

They moved through the carriage until they found four empty seats together – one set of two behind another set of two.

Nat nipped in first and took a window seat. Auntie Bella flopped down next to him.

Sparky and Archie hovered beside the other two seats.

'I really do like sitting by the window,' said Archie. 'In

fact sometimes, if I don't sit by the window, I feel sick.'

Sparky wasn't sure she believed him, but she let him sit next to the window anyway. '*You're* going to have to be the grown-up today,' she could hear Mrs Smart say. And it was the grown-up thing to do.

Sparky listened to the sound of slamming carriage doors. There were still people walking up and down the aisle, searching for empty seats.

Then a whistle blew on the platform outside – and they were off.

Sparky jiggled up and down where she sat. 'I'm so excited, Archie!' Not having a window seat didn't seem to matter anymore.

Auntie Bella half-turned and asked, 'Who'd like a biscuit?' She said it quite loudly so that Sparky and Archie could hear in the seats behind.

A man in a seat on the other side of the aisle looked up and said, 'Ooh, yes please, if you're offering.' Auntie Bella ignored him.

'I'd love a biscuit, please,' said Sparky.

'Me too. Who's got the bag?' Auntie Bella looked at Nat.

Nat gazed out of the window. 'What bag?'

They had just sped past a cow with her head poked through the fence so that she could eat the grass on the other side. Nat hoped her head wasn't stuck.

'You know, the bag,' said Auntie Bella. 'The one with the coats and the snacks and drinks.'

'Don't look at me,' Nat answered.

'Archie, have *you* got the bag?' asked Auntie Bella.

'No,' said Archie. 'I don't remember any bag.'

Sparky could almost hear Auntie Bella grit her teeth. 'I packed a bag,' Auntie Bella said, 'with coats and snacks and drinks. You all saw it. All three of you. Did *none* of you think to pick it up?' She let out a little whimper. 'Oh, please don't tell me it's still in the car!'

'It's still in the car, Mum,' said Nat. He'd lost sight of the munching cow.

'I said don't tell me that!'

Nat shrugged. 'But if it's not on the train, it must be in the car. That's the obvious explanation.'

'I don't remember seeing it in the car,' said Archie.

Sparky didn't remember seeing it in the car either. The last time she'd seen it was on the hall floor at home. But she didn't want to make the situation worse so she said nothing.

'Shame,' said the man in the seat on the other side of the aisle. 'No biscuits for anyone, then.'

Thirty-five minutes later, after three station stops, two trips to the toilet (both Archie) and a lot of huffing and puffing from Auntie Bella, they arrived.

'We're all going to freeze,' grumbled Auntie Bella as she stepped onto the platform. 'Our coats were in that bag.'

The man from the seat on the other side of the aisle stepped off the train after them. 'You're going to go hungry too,' he said as he walked on past, 'because that's where you said your biscuits were.'

'I've got my coat,' said Sparky. 'It wouldn't fit in the bag.'

'It's not even cold,' said Nat.

'Can I have an ice cream?' asked Archie.

Auntie Bella rolled her eyes. 'Let's just go and find this

zoo. And the first thing I'm going to do when we get there is have a very large cup of coffee.'

You'd think a zoo would be easy enough to find. Generally speaking, zoos are quite big with plenty of signs telling you where they are.

But, of course, to find the signs, you have to be on the roads where the signs are. The road from the station wasn't one of those roads. The directions from the lady walking her dog didn't help much either.

Auntie Bella, Nat, Archie and Sparky must have walked in several circles before they finally found the right route. By which time, all Nat and Archie wanted to do was go home because they were tired and hungry. And all Auntie Bella wanted to do was turn back time so she could decide that the zoo was too far away and they could plan a trip to the cinema instead.

Eventually, they found the zoo. The website said it was a ten-minute walk from the station. It took them just over half an hour.

'**They've changed it all!**' complained Auntie Bella as they finally walked in through the tall iron gates. This shouldn't really have come as a surprise. She hadn't been to the zoo for years. 'Why have they changed it all? This isn't what I remember.'

Sparky gazed around, her eyes shining.

'You've changed it all,' Auntie Bella said to the lady selling entry tickets. 'This isn't what I remember.'

'Well, I don't know when you were last here, but we have grown a lot in the last few years,' the ticket seller replied. 'We're running quite a few conservation and education programmes now. And we've got much more space for the animals. It's all very exciting.'

'Is it?' said Auntie Bella. 'This isn't what I remember.'

'*I* think it's exciting.' Sparky beamed at the ticket seller as she took her ticket. 'I've never been here before.'

'Neither have I,' said Archie.

'Don't know if I have or not,' said Nat.

'Well, *I* have,' said Auntie Bella, 'and this isn't what I remember. Now, where can I get a cup of coffee?'

Luckily for Auntie Bella, because the zoo had got bigger, there were now several cafés. The ticket seller gave them a map to help them find their way around. Very helpfully, she put a circle in red biro around each café too. The closest was just round the corner from the main entrance.

As Auntie Bella sipped a large mug of hot, frothy coffee, she checked her phone for messages.

There was a text from Mrs Smart: 'Bella – in case you're wondering where your bag is, you left it here.'

Nat and Sparky munched on crisps and Archie licked an ice cream.

'Please could you text Mum to let her know we've arrived?' asked Sparky.

Auntie Bella dropped her phone back into her bag. 'I'll do it later,' she said.

'Brrr...' Archie huddled into his seat and wrapped his arms around himself. 'I wish you'd brought our coats. I'm freezing.'

Sparky began to wish Stanley was there. This was such an exciting day, but none of the others seemed excited at all.

The first animals they spotted were the zebras. They were in a field, eating grass, just as if they were horses or cows.

Auntie Bella peered at the map of the zoo. 'This isn't what I remember,' she complained. 'And according to this map, those shouldn't be zebras. They should be wallabies.'

'Let me see,' said Nat. Auntie Bella passed him the map. He dropped his head to one side then the other as he studied it. 'No, zebras is right. The wallabies are over there – look.' He pointed.

'You see, this is what happens when people change things.' Auntie Bella pressed a hand to her forehead. 'This isn't what I remember.'

Sparky spotted the word 'meerkats' on the map. 'Let's go and find the meerkats!' she said. And she began to jiggle again. 'I love meerkats, they're so funny.'

'I think we should go and see the rhinoceros first,' said Archie. 'It's supposed to have had a baby.' He'd seen this information on a poster where Auntie Bella had bought their tickets.

'How do you know that?' asked Nat. 'Anyway, I want to see the giraffes. The map says the giraffes are quite close to the elephants and I want to see the elephants too.'

Sparky peered over his shoulder at the map. 'There are giant tortoises! Look!' She jabbed a finger at the area marked 'Giant Tortoises'. 'Oh, can we go there first – *please*?'

Auntie Bella reached out and snatched the map from Nat's fingers. 'I've got a better idea. Let's just go for a walk. If we keep to the path we'll see everything we want to see and I won't have to bother with this silly map.'

There was a litter bin a few steps away. Auntie Bella

marched towards it and dropped the map inside.

Sparky wasn't sure this was a good idea. She also thought that mentioning it was probably even less of a good idea. So she said nothing.

Beyond the zebras were some antelopes. And beyond the antelopes were some ostriches.

When Archie saw them, he started to laugh. 'How can something with such long legs and such a big body have such a tiny head? Where does it keep its brain?'

Nat glanced at him. 'I often wonder that about you.'

As they walked round a corner in the path, it split down the middle and took off in different directions. There were now two ways they could go. One way led to another café, and a sign shaped like a hand with a pointing finger said, 'This way to Baboon Island'. The other way had a sign shaped like a lizard and announced, 'This way to the reptile house'.

'Cool!' cried Nat. 'Let's go and see the lizards!'

Auntie Bella made a face. 'No thanks,' she said as she wrinkled her nose. 'Can't think of anything worse.' The only thing that interested her right at that moment was the café. 'Still, who am I to stop you having fun visiting slimy animals?' she added. 'You three go and enjoy yourselves. I'll be over there having a cup of coffee.'

'Lizards aren't actually slimy,' said Nat.

'Well, they look it,' replied Auntie Bella, 'which is probably worse. Come and find me when you've finished.'

The boys didn't need telling twice. They darted off towards the reptile house without a backward glance. Just as eagerly, Auntie Bella headed for the café.

Sparky hesitated. 'I can't trust Auntie Bella to keep an

eye on *you*,' Mrs Smart had said, 'so it's up to you to make sure you don't lose sight of *her*.'

But Sparky really wanted to visit the reptile house. And when she thought about it, she wasn't exactly losing sight of Auntie Bella. After all, she knew where she'd be.

'Nat! Archie! Wait!' Sparky hurtled after them.

They didn't wait, but she caught up with them in the reptile house anyway.

The reptile house felt much bigger than it looked on the outside. It was hot too and a bit steamy. There were waterways to wander along, tall, leafy plants, and a waterfall that tumbled in front of a high, silvery mirror. When Sparky stood in front of it, she could feel cool splashes of water touch her skin.

There were bridges to cross too, and behind glass panels in their own special spaces were lizards. Lots of them. Some were tiny, others bigger. Some were easy to spot. Others you had to search out because they blended in with their surroundings.

'When something blends in with its surroundings like that, it's called "camel-flage",' said Nat.

'It's not, actually,' replied Archie. 'It's called "camouflage". It's got nothing to do with camels.'

'That's what I said,' answered Nat. '"Camel-flage". And I never mentioned camels.'

'There are camels here,' said Sparky. 'Not in the reptile house but here at the zoo. I saw them on the map.'

'But I never mentioned camels,' said Nat.

Sparky marvelled at the lizards; their colours and shapes and the way some of them flicked out their tongues.

She marvelled at them most of all because it suddenly occurred to her that the same God who'd made lizards had made Nat and Archie, meerkats, giant tortoises *and* camels. And all the other animals at the zoo, for that matter.

I wish my imagination was as big as God's, she thought.

At the far end of the reptile house was another door. A sign over it said 'EXIT' in big letters.

'We don't want to go out that way,' said Sparky.

'Er – yes, we do,' said Archie, 'it says "EXIT".'

'Yes,' Sparky agreed, 'but we need to go out of the door we came in. Otherwise we might not find the café again and we'll lose your mum.'

Archie half raised an eyebrow. It made him look as though the thought of losing his mum didn't bother him especially.

'Of course we'll find her,' said Nat. 'We'll go out of the exit and walk down the side of the building till we get back to where we started – easy.'

'But we might not be able to walk down the side of the building,' Sparky replied. 'It makes much more sense to go out the way we came in.'

Nat and Archie didn't seem to care about being sensible. As Sparky followed them to the exit marked 'EXIT', for the second time that day, she wished Stanley was there.

There wasn't a way down the side of the reptile house. There was a wall. A big, tall, solid wall and there was no way over or around.

'Oh, well.' Nat shrugged his shoulders. 'Let's see where this goes.' And he headed off along a new path with

Archie at his heels.

Sparky was tempted to go back through the reptile house on her own. But the thought of losing sight of Nat and Archie *and* Auntie Bella was a bit much. So she trotted off with reluctant feet after her crinkly-haired cousins.

Their arrival at the meerkat enclosure took her mind off things. But only for a moment. Nat and Archie had spotted a sign to the nocturnal house, and off they went again.

'Wait!' called Sparky, trotting again to keep up. 'I really think we should try to find our way back to Auntie Bella.'

'We will,' said Archie. 'Just as soon as we've checked out the bats. Mum won't want to see the bats.'

'Bats?' Sparky's eyes widened. 'There are bats here too?'

'That's what's in the nocturnal house,' said Archie, 'because they like the night.'

Nat suddenly stopped walking. A thought had just struck him that had nothing to do with bats.

'Do you reckon they let the lions out at the end of the day when everyone goes home?' he asked.

'Do we reckon *who* lets them out?' Archie replied.

'The zoo-keepers,' said Nat.

Sparky frowned. 'Why would they do that?'

'I don't know, but they might,' said Nat. 'Who knows what they do when there's no one here? I'm sure I've heard that, though.'

'You haven't!' scoffed Archie.

'I might have,' answered Nat.

The nocturnal house was pitch black inside – so black that it was quite a shock stepping in from the broad daylight outside.

'I can't see a thing!' Sparky gasped. 'This is darker than anywhere I've ever been!'

Sparky wasn't sure she liked it. She wasn't all that keen on the dark at home, but at least it *was* home. At Priory Park, she knew what was what and where was where, in the dark or the light.

There could be anything in the blackness here. Anything at all. And it smelt funny...

'Nat... Archie... Where are you...?'

'I see one!' hissed Nat. 'A bat – I see one!'

As Sparky's eyes grew a little more used to the darkness, she thought she could just about make out the shadowy shapes of Nat and Archie. They stood at the glass that separated visitors from the creatures behind it.

She went to step towards them when something brushed past her leg.

'Eek!' A surprised squeal escaped from Sparky's lips even though she didn't want it to. And she froze.

'Mollie!' A woman's voice called through the blackness. 'Mollie, come back here right now and hold my hand!'

The thing that had brushed past Sparky's leg turned out to be a small child – not the creepy, dark-dwelling creature with scary-looking claws and even scarier-looking teeth that Sparky had imagined. The small child brushed back past Sparky's leg and ran towards her mum's voice.

Sparky felt slightly disappointed with herself. Mollie may only be little, but that small girl was far braver than she was.

'Nat, Archie, I'm coming over.' Sparky stretched out her

arms. If she was going to bump into something, she'd rather do it hands first.

Neither Nat nor Archie answered. Sparky stopped and peered towards the bat enclosure. The shadowy shapes she'd taken to be her cousins didn't seem to be there anymore. She walked forward a few more steps until her fingers touched the glass panel.

The longer she was in the nocturnal house, the more her eyes got used to the dark and the more she could see. For instance, she could now make out a bat... two bats... no, three... They hung, wings folded, upside down from a branch.

Wow! Sparky thought. *Is there no end to God's imagination?*

What Sparky couldn't see, however, was Nat and Archie.

'Nat... Archie... Stop messing about, I know you're in here...'

No answer.

'Stop mucking about right now,' Sparky said. 'You're not funny. I know you wouldn't leave me in here on my own.'

But although Sparky said, 'I know you wouldn't leave me in here on my own,' she was beginning to suspect that that's exactly what Nat and Archie had done.

'Look, where are you?' Sparky tried again. 'Can you not do this, please? You might only be playing around but I don't actually like it.'

There was silence. Nothing. Just Mollie and her mum shuffling about in the shadows. And that funny smell.

I wish Stanley was here, Sparky thought, for the third time that day. Stanley would never have left her on her own in the nocturnal house. Not even for a joke. Stanley never played jokes. He didn't have a sense of humour.

'Look, Mollie,' Mollie's mum said suddenly. 'Look at the pretty bat.'

Mollie didn't seem to care. 'Want to go now,' she replied.

Sparky could see the shapes of Mollie and her mum move past her. Thinking quickly, and not wanting to be left by herself with the bats, however well she could now see, she decided to follow them.

There was a thick rubber flap at one end of the building. Sparky caught it as Mollie's mum flicked it back to let Mollie run through and make her own way out. Sparky slipped out behind the two of them.

It was a little brighter on the other side. And there in front of her was the door to the outside, marked 'EXIT'.

When Sparky stepped back out into the daylight, it was almost as much of a shock as stepping into the pitch black. She had to blink and squint into the brightness.

She fully expected to hear Nat and Archie burst into giggles.

'I don't care,' she got ready to say. 'It's not like I'm scared of the dark. Or bats, or anything.'

But there was no giggling because there was no Nat and Archie.

Still blinking, Sparky began to walk along the path that led away from the nocturnal house. Mollie and her mum were almost out of sight.

Some other children ran towards her.

'Don't get lost!' a man called. Sparky thought he must be their dad. He passed her by and hurried after them.

That's when she realised.

The way she'd left the nocturnal house wasn't the way she'd gone in. She was now in a different part of the zoo.

Nothing looked familiar.

There weren't meerkats along this path. There were no signs for the reptile house. Nat and Archie were nowhere to be seen. In fact, there was nothing Sparky recognised. And as for Auntie Bella in her café, for all Sparky knew, she'd given up on all three of them and caught the train home!

Oh, no... Sparky thought as it dawned on her. *I'm lost! For the first time in my whole life ever... I'm really, truly lost.*

Because Sparky was usually so good at churning out bright ideas, there wasn't much she got in a panic about. If there was a problem, she could usually rely on her brain to come up with some sort of solution. Sometimes, if they asked her to, Sparky would come up with solutions to other people's problems too. And she'd regularly try to solve Stanley's difficulties, whether he asked her to or not.

Being lost at the zoo, however – all on her own and surrounded by strangers – was possibly Sparky's biggest challenge yet.

She began to feel a bit odd: cold all over but slightly sweaty at the same time. Her heart was doing an unusual thuddy sort of thing and she felt a bit sick. However, she decided the sick feeling could be because she was hungry, not because she was in a panic. She might have been all alone and lost in a big zoo she'd never been to before, but it *was* nearly lunchtime and she'd only eaten a bag of crisps since breakfast.

Besides, Sparky thought to herself, *if Nat and Archie aren't on this side of the nocturnal house, they must be on the other side. So the thing is, all I've got to do is go back through the bats and I'll find them.*

But going back through the bats (into the thick, black

darkness with the strange smell) was the last thing Sparky wanted to do.

She lifted a thumb to her mouth and began to gnaw on the nail. *The other thing is,* she thought, *Auntie Bella won't have left me and got the train home, because even* she *cares about me too much to do that. And God cares about me too much to let that happen.*

Sparky sucked in a deep breath and turned away from the nocturnal house.

'Come on,' she murmured. 'You're Sparky Smart from Priory Park. You can do this. Pull your socks up and pull yourself together.' She could imagine Mrs Smart talking to herself like that if she were lost at a zoo.

Then Sparky made a plan.

If she kept walking, she felt sure she'd (probably) see another sign for the nocturnal house. If she followed the sign, she'd (probably) end up round the other side of the building where Nat and Archie would (probably) still be waiting for her.

And if Nat and Archie *weren't* waiting for her, she'd keep walking until she saw a sign for the reptile house. If she went back to the reptile house, she'd (probably) find the café where they'd all left Auntie Bella, and Auntie Bella would (probably) still be there drinking coffee.

As Sparky set off, she did her best to ignore the fact that there were several 'probably's in her plan and not a single 'definitely'.

'If it's got a "probably" in it, it's not much of a plan at all,' Stanley would have said... probably.

As Sparky walked, she saw signs for the giraffes and

signs for the elephants. She also saw signs for something called a capybara. What a capybara was, she had no clue.

Perhaps it's a type of bear, she thought. *Or a sort of whale. Or I suppose it might be something really, really tiny like an ant.*

For your information, a capybara isn't a bear or a whale or an ant. It looks a bit like a guinea pig with quite long legs. Now you know more than Sparky does because she's *in* this story, not reading it like you.

Next, Sparky spotted a sign that read: 'This way to the big cats!'

Sparky assumed that 'big cats' must have meant lions and tigers and cheetahs – not cats like Monday, Tuesday and Thursday, who belonged to Miss Clatworthy next door. They weren't very big at all.

Suddenly, she stopped dead. Her breathing froze for a moment too.

What was that Nat had said? 'Do you reckon they let the lions out at the end of the day when everyone goes home?'

Sparky's face went pale. Of course, Sparky couldn't see her own face, but if someone else had seen it, they might have said, 'Goodness, you do look pale.'

Her heart began to do the thuddy thing again too.

'But I'm *bound* to find Nat and Archie or Auntie Bella before the end of the day,' she whispered to herself. Instead of chewing on her thumb nail, this time she started to chew her lower lip. 'And if they *do* let the lions out when everyone goes home, Auntie Bella will be *bound* to tell them to wait until I've gone home too.'

Sparky tried to put herself in a lion's shoes. (Not

literally, obviously. When was the last time you saw a lion wearing shoes?) If she were a lion and happened to bump into a smallish girl who looked a lot like Sparky, would she think the smallish, Sparky-like girl looked good enough to eat? Or would she turn up her nose and go in search of someone bigger and less scrawny-looking – someone like Auntie Bella, for instance? Or Nat and Archie who, both together, would probably be far more filling?

Luckily, at that moment, the quick-thinking part of Sparky's brain kicked in and told her not to be so silly. What kind of zoo would let their lions out at *any* time of day?

Still, as she started along the path again, she decided it wouldn't hurt to keep a look out. She imagined that Auntie Bella would be in more than enough trouble if Mrs Smart ever found out she'd lost Sparky even for a short while. How much more trouble would she be in if she let Sparky get eaten by a lion?

'*You're* going to have to be the grown-up,' she told herself, just as Mrs Smart had told her that morning. '*You're* going to have to be the one to look out for lions.' Not that Mrs Smart had said a word about lions, but Sparky was sure she would have done had she thought there was any chance of the lion-keepers letting them out.

As Sparky neared the end of this particular path, she saw something that made her thuddy heart leap.

'A map of the zoo!' She was so relieved, she did one of her little jiggles of excitement. An elderly couple who happened to be passing at that moment gave her a hard stare.

The map was in a large metal frame, fixed to posts.

Now I'll be able to see exactly where I am, Sparky

thought as she bounced towards it.

Have you ever stood in front of one of those big maps in places like zoos and theme parks? They usually have a large arrow and the words '**YOU ARE HERE**' printed helpfully at the point on the map where you're standing.

However, knowing YOU ARE HERE doesn't necessarily mean you'll be able to read the map and get to where you want to be. Especially if you haven't had much practice at reading maps. Which Sparky hadn't.

'If Stanley was here,' Sparky muttered to herself, 'he'd be able to read this map, no problem.' And for the fourth time that day, she wished that he was.

'Sparky! Sparky, that is you, isn't it?'

Sparky was so surprised by the voice that boomed out quite close to her ear that she almost fell into the map head first.

She managed to recover her balance and turned

towards the voice. And her mouth dropped open so wide that anyone who walked past could easily have seen her tonsils, had they chosen to have a look.

'Mrs Obi!'

Mrs Obi, her husband Mr Obi, baby Eric and their little dog Minnie lived next door to the Smarts on Priory Park. Mr Obi sometimes went running with Mr Smart.

In front of Mrs Obi, Baby Eric sat in his buggy and stared at Sparky. He was sucking a shoe. (Don't worry – it was one of his own tiny shoes that he must have pulled off his foot, not one of Mr Obi's large, stinky running trainers.) Minnie was there too, panting at the end of her lead.

Mr Obi seemed to have stayed at home.

'What are *you* doing here?' Sparky was staring as wide-eyed as Eric.

'I could ask you the same question,' replied Mrs Obi. 'Is your mum here too?' She glanced around. 'I wish I'd known. We could have all gone in the same car.'

'Actually, I didn't come in the car,' Sparky said. 'I came on the train.'

'Did you indeed?' Mrs Obi raised an eyebrow. 'Very fancy.'

'Oh, I wasn't trying to be fancy,' Sparky answered. 'It was just that Auntie Bella didn't think she'd find the zoo in the car.'

Mrs Obi reached down and gently pulled baby Eric's tiny shoe out of his little mouth. 'I see. So you're here with your Auntie Bella?'

The moment Sparky had let slip the words 'Auntie Bella', she wished she hadn't. If Mrs Obi believed Sparky was here with Mrs Smart, Sparky would have been happy for her to carry on believing that. She could pretend that Mrs Smart wasn't there right at that moment because she'd taken Sissy to buy an ice cream. Or to the toilet.

'I'm just waiting here on my own because I like looking at maps,' Sparky could have said. 'You carry on looking round the zoo, Mrs Obi, because I don't know how long Mum will be. But I'll tell her I saw you and who knows? We might bump into you again.'

However, Mrs Obi now knew Sparky was at the zoo with Auntie Bella. Or rather that Sparky was at the zoo – and Auntie Bella was nowhere in sight. And if Mrs Obi found out that Auntie Bella had somehow lost Sparky, then Mrs Smart was bound to find out too, which would lead to all sorts of trouble.

'Where is she then?' Mrs Obi had another look around her. 'Where is your Auntie Bella?'

As quick-thinking as she was, on this occasion, Sparky wasn't quick-thinking enough to fool Mrs Obi.

'Well... the thing is...' Sparky hesitated. She didn't think it would work if she said Auntie Bella had taken Nat and Archie to the toilet.

'The thing is...' And if Auntie Bella had gone with Nat and Archie to buy ice creams, why wouldn't Sparky have gone too?

'The thing really is...'

'Sparky,' Mrs Obi interrupted and asked again, '*where* is your Auntie Bella?'

Sparky looked at her feet. There was no escape. She'd have to tell the truth. 'The thing is, the last time I saw her, she was having a cup of coffee... And then I got lost in the bat house. But please – *please* –' Sparky added, 'you mustn't tell Mum! I'm only a little bit lost. Not a lot lost. And now that I've found a map,' – she pointed to the map in the frame behind her – 'I'll be able to find myself again really quickly!'

Mrs Obi's eyes narrowed. 'But that map's not going to tell you where your Auntie Bella is, is it?'

'It's *my* fault really. I went out of the bat house by the wrong door. So then I couldn't find Nat and Archie.'

'Nat and Archie?' Both eyebrows on Mrs Obi's face shot upwards. 'Do you mean Nat and Archie are lost at the zoo too?'

Sparky's shoulders sank. 'I'm not really sure,' she said. 'But I think they might be.'

Mrs Obi shook her head.

Poor Auntie Bella, Sparky thought. *She's going to be in so much trouble.*

* * * *

Had Sparky been able to see Auntie Bella at that moment, she would have known that her aunt's troubles had already begun.

As she sat at her café table and enjoyed her third cup of coffee that morning, Auntie Bella had realised that Nat, Archie and Sparky had been gone quite a while. To begin with, she'd thought, *Well, it must be a very big reptile house. I only hope it isn't full of very big reptiles...*

But it wasn't until sometime later that Auntie Bella began to seriously wonder where the twins and Sparky had got to. They'd been gone ages. However big the reptile house was, it couldn't be *that* big.

She glanced at her watch. Seeing the time didn't help because she hadn't checked what the time was when they'd set off. She wished she had. There was no way of knowing exactly how long they'd been gone but by now, one thing was clear: however long it was, it was too long.

Auntie Bella stood up and gave the reptile house an angry glare. 'Typical. You take the family on the train for a nice day out, you give them your undivided attention, and what happens?' she muttered to herself. 'They disappear on you. Well, charming is all I can say. **Absolutely charming!**'

Another few moments passed. There were children all around. Every time Auntie Bella heard a shout or a laugh, she turned to look. But none of these children were the ones she was waiting for.

No – it was becoming clear that she would have to take action.

The problem was, the action she would have to take meant going into the reptile house. That, Auntie Bella assumed, was where Nat, Archie and Sparky were messing about. And that was the last place at the zoo Auntie Bella wanted to visit.

'Reptiles,' she murmured with a shudder. 'Nasty, slithery, slimy, horrible things,' and she began to walk towards the entrance.

Inside her head, Auntie Bella pictured the most hideous-looking creatures: little green monsters with flat feet, spiky heads, sticky-out ears and dribbly mouths. All in all, nothing like the reptiles in the reptile house.

Taking a deep breath, she pushed on the door. 'When I get my hands on Nat and Archie, there's going to be big trouble...'

As Auntie Bella stepped inside, the steamy heat of the reptile house hit her. Auntie Bella hated the heat. She didn't like the cold much either, but she hated the heat more. The further in she walked, the hotter she got. She fished around in her handbag for a tissue and began to dab at her face.

'Kids!' she hissed to herself. 'This is the last time I take them *anywhere, ever*!'

Auntie Bella ignored the lizards all around her – she couldn't bear the thought of actually seeing one – and kept her eyes fixed straight ahead. But no matter how much she searched, Nat, Archie and Sparky were nowhere to be found.

Finally, Auntie Bella shoved her way through the exit at the far end. She gulped in the fresh, cool outside air. She dabbed furiously at her hot, flushed face.

She looked all around in the vain hope that her missing family might pop out of the ground and shout, 'Surprise!'

But they didn't. Obviously.

'Are you all right? You don't look very well.' A man stood in front of her. He wore grey trousers and a green shirt with 'Zoo' embroidered on the front pocket. 'Can I get you anything? Do you need to sit down?'

Auntie Bella began to wail: '**Noooo!**'

The wail had been building inside her. She'd been trying to keep it under control but now it escaped at full volume.

It screeched through the air, rather like the squeals of the baboons on Baboon Island when they got over-excited.

'I don't want water! Why would I want water? I'm looking for three children! I've lost them! Three of them – and one of them's not even mine! Noooo!'

The man, who worked at the zoo and looked after the animals (which is why he had 'Zoo' on his shirt), looked a little taken aback. He was used to wailing children. A wailing grown-up, however, was a bit more of a challenge. And this particular wailing grown-up was creating quite a hullabaloo.

'Erm... there, there,' he said. He thought about patting Auntie Bella on the head but decided against it. 'They won't have got far. I'm sure you don't need to worry.'

'Worry?' Auntie Bella began to sob. 'I'm not worried, I'm absolutely furious!'

This wasn't strictly true. Auntie Bella *was* worried. Very worried. But because she usually only worried about herself, worrying about other people was something of a new sensation. She wasn't quite sure how to cope with it.

Luckily, for people like Auntie Bella who accidentally lose their children – and for children like Sparky, Nat and Archie who accidentally lose their grown-ups – the zoo had a plan.

The losers and the lost could go to an office near the main ticket desk. There, they could give the names of the people they needed to find, which would be announced over loud speakers throughout the zoo. If all went to plan, a short while afterwards, they'd all be safely reunited.

'Oh, yes,' said the zoo man as he ushered Auntie Bella

through the door of the office. 'I've seen many families brought happily back together at this very spot. Were you not given a map when you came in? Everything you need to know about getting lost is on there...'

Auntie Bella sat on a chair by the desk. She didn't bother to mention that, yes, she had been given a map, but she'd thrown it away.

The zoo man wasted no time in making the announcement. He made it several times, just to be sure.

'Now what?' said Auntie Bella.

'Now, we wait,' the zoo man replied.

The waiting was a little longer than the zoo man thought it might be. That's because it took Nat and Archie quite a while to find their way back to the main entrance and the ticket desk.

But at last, they appeared in the office doorway.

'There you are, you see,' said the zoo man. He looked pleased with himself – and somewhat relieved. 'Fool proof. It's as simple as that.'

'Where *have* you been?' Auntie Bella shot up out of her seat. 'I've been looking everywhere! I had to walk all through that reptile house, which was the *last* thing I wanted to do – nasty, slithery, slimy, horrible things – and there was no sign of you! Why didn't you come straight back? Where did you go? What...' Auntie Bella's voice trailed away.

Her eyes flicked beyond Nat and Archie to the empty space behind them.

'Wait a minute,' she began again, 'there's only two of you. Where's the other one?' Her eyes went wide and a bit wild and her voice rose to a shriek. 'WHAT HAVE YOU DONE WITH SPARKY?'

Once again, the zoo man looked uncomfortable.

Nat looked uncomfortable too. 'I don't know,' he mumbled. 'We were all in the bat house. Then Archie and I left and Sparky didn't.'

Archie looked outraged. 'You *told* us to leave! You said to sneak off and leave Sparky in there for a joke!'

'I did not!' Nat snapped.

'You so did!'

'Did not!'

'Did!'

'ENOUGH!' screamed Auntie Bella. 'I don't care who did what when. All I want to know is – **WHERE IS SPARKY NOW?**'

'She's right here,' said a quiet voice. It belonged to Mrs Obi.

Auntie Bella spun round. Sparky stood in the office doorway, holding Mrs Obi's hand.

* * * *

'I'm glad you had a lovely day, Sparky,' Mrs Smart whispered when she went up to say goodnight. She didn't want to disturb Sissy, who was fast asleep in the other bed.

'I did, thank you,' replied Sparky. 'It was very... exciting. Nat says they let the lions out after everyone goes home. But I don't think that can be right, can it?'

Mrs Smart blinked at her. 'No, Sparky. No, I don't think it can.'

'Night, then,' said Sparky. She went to turn over but Mrs

Smart hadn't finished.

'So, everything went smoothly, did it?'

'Uh-huh,' Sparky answered. 'Pretty smoothly.'

'Pretty smoothly?' Mrs Smart gave her a searching look. 'Nothing went wrong at all? Because Auntie Bella was very quiet when she dropped you home. Much quieter than usual. She didn't complain about a single thing.'

'Well,' said Sparky, 'that just goes to show what a good day it was.'

'Hmm...' Mrs Smart looked thoughtful. 'And while you were getting ready for bed, guess who popped round? Mrs Obi.'

Sparky's eyes stretched just a little bit wide. 'Did she? That's nice.'

'You didn't mention that Mrs Obi was at the zoo today with Eric and Minnie.'

'Didn't I?' Sparky wished she could pull her duvet over her head. 'I must have forgotten.'

'She says she ran into you there,' Mrs Smart continued, 'and she hopes you've recovered from your adventure.'

'Did she?' Sparky said again. 'That's nice.'

Mrs Smart smiled. 'Yes, isn't it?' She paused. 'So what adventure would that be, Sparky?'

Sparky's quick-thinking brain was struggling again. 'Well, it's quite an adventure going on the train to the zoo.'

Mrs Smart nodded. 'Yes, it is. But not really the sort of adventure you'd need to recover from – is it?'

No, Sparky supposed it wasn't.

In the other bed, Sissy sucked in a long, deep breath and kicked off her covers. Sparky hoped she'd wake up and distract Mrs Smart.

She didn't.

Sparky thought back to the moment she and Auntie Bella had been reunited. Auntie Bella had flung her arms around Sparky and given her the biggest hug Sparky had ever had from her auntie.

She'd grabbed Nat and Archie too and pulled them to her, her arms almost bursting with the three of them crushed inside.

'I thought I'd lost you for good,' Auntie Bella had sobbed. 'How could I live with myself if I lost any of you? I should never have let you wander off on your own. I'm sorry. I'm so, so sorry!' And she'd held them so tightly, they'd struggled to breathe.

'The thing is, Mum,' Sparky began, 'I didn't get eaten by a lion. So that can only be a good thing.'

'A very good thing,' Mrs Smart agreed.

'And if something *had* happened and Auntie Bella *had* stayed in the café to have a cup of coffee while me, Nat and Archie went to the reptile house on our own... and if we *had* gone out of the reptile house through the other door and found the bat house... and if Nat and Archie *had* sneaked out and left me all by myself with the bats... and if I then couldn't find them *or* Auntie Bella because I was lost at the zoo... none of that makes Auntie Bella a bad person, does it?'

The frown that made a crease between Mrs Smart's eyebrows was growing deeper and deeper.

'It's like I said this morning,' Sparky went on, 'if God made people to be like Him, then Auntie Bella *must*

be like Him. He's just waiting for her to be His friend so that He can polish up that special part inside her. In any case,' she added, 'God's always ready to give us a second chance, isn't He? He's the King of second chances – that's what Grandad says. And if God would give Auntie Bella a second chance, then so should we.'

Mrs Smart's frown relaxed a little and her eyebrows lifted. She wondered if second chances applied to trips to the zoo.

'We all make mistakes sometimes – I'm sure I make loads. And God always forgives us,' Sparky said. 'So that means we should forgive each other.'

In bed at the other end of the room, Sissy rolled over and her covers slipped to the floor.

'Forgibbee chudder...' she murmured.

Escape of the mouse-creature

'All right, Stanley, joke's over. You've got till I count to ten. One... two...'

Mr Smart had been waiting to get into the bathroom for 20 minutes. 'I'm not joking, Stanley, so I hope you're taking me seriously... three... four...'

The wait probably wouldn't have mattered quite so much to Mr Smart if it had been the first time this week. But it wasn't. Mr Smart had been made to wait and wait for Stanley to finish in the bathroom on Tuesday, Wednesday, Thursday and now Friday. He wasn't amused.

'I'm warning you, Stanley... eight... nine... Last

chance... TEN.'

Mr Smart spat out the number 'ten' through clenched teeth.

'All right, all right,' Stanley mumbled from the other side of the door.

Mr Smart heard the lock click. Which was just as well. Because no matter how serious he was about Stanley coming out of the bathroom, if Stanley *hadn't* come out, there wasn't a lot he could have done about it.

Mr Smart eyed his son as he sloped past. 'What have you been doing in there all this time? Planting a tree?'

'I've been getting ready for school,' grunted Stanley. 'Like I do every morning.'

'You don't always spend an hour in the bathroom just to get ready for school,' said Mr Smart.

Stanley sighed. 'It wasn't an hour. No one spends an hour in the bathroom getting ready for school.'

'Well, it felt like an hour,' Mr Smart grumbled. He ducked into the bathroom and locked the door. 'Nearly every day this week, Stanley. An hour nearly every day this week!'

'The thing is, though,' Sparky said to Mr Smart in the kitchen at the end of the day, 'don't you wonder *why* Stanley's spending an hour in the bathroom before school?'

'No.' Mr Smart shook his head. 'I just wish he'd stop it.'

'But don't you think you *should* wonder?' Sparky said.

Mr Smart made a face. 'Why?'

'Because it's a mystery,' Sparky insisted. 'And mysteries need solving.'

'The only mystery,' said Mr Smart, 'is that Stanley's being selfish. He can't keep hogging the bathroom every day of the week just because he feels like it. It's not on.'

Why is it, Sparky wondered, that grown-ups so often miss the point? This had nothing to do with selfishness or hogging, or even days of the week, for that matter.

Something was going on. And if something was going on, it was up to someone to find out what it was. Since Mr Smart wasn't interested and Mrs Smart was probably too busy to care about Stanley's bathroom habits (because she was having such a long term), Sparky knew it was up to her.

On Saturday morning, the first thing Sparky noticed was that Stanley didn't spend an hour in the bathroom. He hardly spent any time in the bathroom at all. In fact, his time in the bathroom was so short, Sparky would have been surprised if he'd had time to comb his hair, let alone wash his face and brush his teeth.

'Interesting,' Sparky said to herself.

She wrote her discovery down in her small 'investigator's' notebook. (It was a notebook she'd found in a kitchen drawer. The only other note-type books she had were her school exercise books. She decided that Mr Barber, her teacher, might not be too happy about her using one of those to write about Stanley's bathroom habits.)

On Sunday morning, Stanley spent a little longer in the bathroom than on Saturday morning. But that was because the family were all going to church. How much Stanley washed on a Saturday was his own business. But Mrs Smart made it *her* business on a Sunday. If they were going to turn up to church together, a clean face was the very least she expected.

'Interesting but normal,' Sparky wrote in her investigator's notebook.

On Monday morning, Stanley spent a long time in the bathroom yet again. So long that Mr Smart grumbled, 'If this doesn't stop soon, one of us is going to have to move out.'

'Well, it's not going to be me,' Stanley muttered, far too quietly for Mr Smart to hear.

It didn't stop there. When Sparky went downstairs for breakfast, she heard Stanley ask Mrs Smart, 'You're sure I look all right?'

'You look fine, Stanley – why?' replied Mrs Smart.

'No reason,' said Stanley. But then he went and checked himself in the hall mirror. He even did a bit of hair-smoothing!

Sparky shot upstairs to make a note of all these things.

She'd crack this mystery if it was the last thing she did.

After school that afternoon, as usual, Sparky walked home with Grandad.

'Grandad?' Sparky said. 'Have you noticed anything strange about Stanley?'

Grandad raised a bushy eyebrow. 'What do you mean by "strange"?' he asked.

'I don't mean strange as in normal for Stanley but strange for most other people,' Sparky answered. 'You know – like disappearing for hours on end to your bedroom so you can write the weather forecast. I mean strange as in unusual, even for Stanley.'

Grandad's other bushy eyebrow slid up to join the first one. 'Unusual,' he said. 'Well, let me think.' Grandad tapped on his chin with his fingers. 'Actually, now you come to mention it, we did have rather an unusual conversation last week.'

Sparky's eyes shone. 'Did you?!' she cried. 'I knew it! I knew something mysterious was going on!' She pulled her rucksack off her shoulders and fished around inside for her investigator's notebook. 'You've got to tell me exactly what Stanley said, Grandad. Word for word.'

'I'm not sure I can remember *exactly* what he said,' Grandad replied.

'But you've got to try!' Sparky insisted. 'So that I can write it all down.' She pulled a pencil out of her rucksack too.

Grandad's eyebrows dropped into a frown. 'Are you sure you can write while we're walking along? Wouldn't it be better to wait until we get home?'

'Of course I can write and walk. I can do anything when I really want to. Come on, just tell me what he said.'

'Well,' Grandad began, 'he asked me about Verity.'

Verity Pringle lived just down the road from Grandad. They were great friends. Mrs Pringle often helped Grandad to water his garden and the plants in his greenhouse. She wasn't much of a gardener herself but she loved listening to Grandad talk about his prize-winning tomatoes.

'Yes, but what did he actually say?' said Sparky. She was getting just the tiniest bit impatient.

'He said, "Grandad, can I ask you about Verity?"' Grandad replied.

Sparky waited expectantly. '**And?**'

'I said he could ask whatever he wanted.'

'Yes, but *what* did he ask?!' Sometimes conversations were enough to make your head explode.

'He wanted to know what we liked doing together and I said, "Ballroom dancing".'

It was Sparky's turn to frown, but she scribbled 'ballroom dancing' down anyway.

'I didn't know you and Mrs Pringle go ballroom dancing,' she said.

'To be honest,' Grandad replied, 'we don't so much as do it as sit down together and watch it on the TV.'

'And what else do you like doing?' Sparky asked.

'Verity's quite taken with my crochet classes. She's very good too. She's making a bed jacket.'

A bed jacket is a jacket someone might wear in bed so they don't cold get while sitting up and reading. But this wasn't the picture that popped into Sparky's head. She imagined a bed wearing a jacket.

'Verity also very much enjoys my singing,' Grandad went on. 'She loves it when I burst into song in the greenhouse. She once told me my singing is one of her favourite things about me.'

Sparky busily scribbled down every word.

'Then Stanley asked,' Grandad added, '"Do all ladies like being sung to and, if so, could you teach me how to sing?"'

This was such a strange request for Stanley that Sparky almost dropped her pencil.

'And what did *you* say?' she asked.

'I said, "I think you'll find that rather depends on the lady."'

'And what did Stanley say?'

'Erm...' Grandad did more tapping of his fingers on his chin. 'He said, "Oh", I think.'

'Oh...' said Sparky.

'But the strangest part of the conversation was this: Stanley said, "When you met Grandma, did you know she was the one?" "The one what?" I asked. "You know," he said, "the *one*. The one you wanted to marry. Your forever person."'

This time, Sparky did drop her pencil. She almost dropped her notebook too, and she certainly had to stop walking.

Suddenly, everything fell into place.

'That's it, Grandad!'

'What's it?' Grandad replied.

'*That!*' Sparky was beside herself with excitement at her own cleverness. 'Stanley's taking ages in the bathroom on school days. Not at the weekend. Just on school days. He's been asking Mum if he looks all right *and* he checks himself in the mirror before he leaves the house. You know what this means, Grandad, don't you?'

'Do I?' said Grandad.

'Yes!' Sparky exploded. '**Stanley's in love!**'

'Is he now?' Grandad replied. He didn't seem nearly as surprised as Sparky thought he should be by her announcement. Nor did he seem especially impressed by her cleverness.

'Grandad, did you hear what I said?'

'I did,' Grandad said.

'Is that all? Just "I did"? Aren't you the littlest, tiniest bit surprised?'

'Not really.' Grandad shook his head.

'But WHY NOT?'

Grandad shrugged his shoulders. 'Because Stanley told me.'

* * * *

Sparky was quiet at dinner.

'You're quiet,' said Mrs Smart. 'What's up?'

'Nothing,' Sparky answered.

Mr Smart finished crunching on a piece of celery. 'You're very quiet for nothing to be up. So what's up?'

'Nothing,' Sparky said again. She threw Stanley an accusing glare. 'Why would anything be up?'

Stanley looked puzzled. 'What have *I* done?'

Sparky stared at him. 'It's what you *haven't* done that's the problem, Stanley. Why don't you think about that for a minute?'

Mr and Mrs Smart exchanged a glance.

Sissy picked up her celery and threw it on the floor.

'I don't know what you're talking about,' said Stanley.

Sparky narrowed her eyes. 'Oh, but you will, Stanley. Later, you *so* will...'

When Stanley went up to his room after dinner, he was surprised to walk in and find Sparky had beaten him to it.

'Why are you in my room?' he demanded.

'Why have you fallen in love and not even mentioned it to me?'

Stanley was shocked. So shocked, he couldn't speak. Then, when he did recover enough to say something, whatever it was he wanted to say was lost in a splutter.

Sparky stared at him. 'Pardon?' she said.

'I'm not...' Stanley tried again. 'I haven't... I wouldn't... I can't...' He sucked in a long breath. 'What's it got to do with you anyway?'

Sparky's stare became a glare. 'I live with you, Stanley. It's got everything to do with me.'

'But I'm not in love! Why would you think that?'

'Because I'm clever, Stanley.' Sparky folded her arms. 'I worked it out.'

Stanley turned in the doorway and glanced towards the landing. There was no one around. Mr and Mrs Smart and Sissy were still downstairs. He closed his bedroom door anyway.

'What I want to know is,' Sparky demanded, 'why wouldn't you tell me something like that?'

Stanley thrust his hands into his pockets. 'But why

would I tell you? It's not like you can help or anything. You've never been in love,' Stanley argued. 'Not that I'm saying I am!' he added quickly.

Sparky's jaw dropped. 'What do you mean I can't help? I'm the most helpful person in this family. The most helpful person on Priory Park. *And* I'm the one with the best ideas!'

Stanley looked doubtful. Sparky did have lots of ideas but they weren't always the best.

There was the time one of Miss Clatworthy's cats had found its way into the Smarts' house through a window. Stanley had found it fast asleep in his bedroom, curled up on his favourite pair of socks.

'Look at them – they're covered in cat hair!' he'd cried in a dismal voice, once he'd managed to rescue them.

'I've got an idea!' Sparky had said. 'Let's hoover them.'

The cat hair had stayed stuck to the socks. The socks had ended up inside the hoover.

Then there was the time the sole had started to come away from the bottom of one of Stanley's shoes.

'I've got an idea!' Sparky had said. 'We'll glue it.'

Sparky had found some glue in Mr Smart's tool kit. 'Perfect,' she'd said. 'It says on the tube it's quick-drying.'

She'd squirted plenty out to make sure it worked. And had then added a few squirts more to make extra sure.

The sole had stuck to the shoe perfectly. Unfortunately, when Stanley put the shoe on a short while later, his foot had got stuck too.

Stanley flopped down onto his bed. As he did so, he sighed heavily. So heavily that Sparky wasn't entirely sure if the noise had come from Stanley or from his mattress.

She waited a moment, then plonked down next to him. 'You know I can help you, Stanley,' she said. 'All you have to do is ask.'

Stanley had to admit that, even though Sparky's ideas sometimes didn't go to plan, she did have a huge heart.

Sparky had once said she'd like to have a heart as huge as God's because she wanted to be able to love people as much as He did. But she knew she had a long, long way to go. Step one, she'd decided, was to try to have a heart as big as Grandad's.

'There's a girl in my class,' Stanley said. 'Her name's Roselle.'

'That's a nice name,' Sparky replied. She wriggled about on the bed to make herself comfortable; the way Sissy did when Sparky read her a bedtime story.

'She moved to our school last term and although she's in my class, I wasn't really that interested in her before,' Stanley continued.

'Before what?' asked Sparky.

'Before the project.'

For the last few weeks, Stanley had been as happy as he'd ever been at school. One of his teachers had announced that the class project for this half of term was to be about the weather.

They would investigate all sorts of weather: gales, thunderstorms, hurricanes, typhoons, tornadoes. They'd look at different levels of rainfall around the world, and when and where snow was most likely. And they'd discover stories of the largest ever hail stones that had fallen in the scariest ever hailstorms.

Stanley lived for the weather. He'd spend hours in his bedroom studying forecasts. He'd fill up countless notebooks with his weather scribbles. He'd write his own weather forecasts and his ambition was to one day be a TV weatherperson.

So, a whole-school project all about the weather was, for him, a dream come true.

Stanley didn't expect anyone else in his class to care much about the project. After all, not even his family at Priory Park got especially excited about the weather.

He was therefore completely bowled over by Roselle's enthusiasm. When the teacher had made the announcement, Roselle had clapped her hands together and cried, 'What a fantastic project!'

Roselle sat two rows in front of Stanley. He'd spent almost the whole of the rest of that lesson staring at the back of her head.

'This is it, Stanley!' Sparky exploded, as Stanley finished explaining why Roselle was so special. 'You've found a girl who likes weather! She's perfect for you. **You're going to have to marry her!**'

Stanley leapt off the bed. 'You see? I knew I shouldn't have told you. I knew you'd make it... stupid!'

Sparky leapt off the bed too. 'I'm not making it stupid, Stanley. Don't you see? You might never meet another girl in the whole of your life who cares about the weather as much as you do. You and Roselle are made for each other!'

'Huh...' Stanley grunted. 'You can only be made for each other if you both like each other. And Roselle just isn't interested in me. Most of the time, she doesn't even know I'm there.'

He sank back down onto the bed.

Sparky dropped down next to him. 'That's why you need a plan. And that's why,' she added, with a glint in her eye, 'I'm going to help you make one.'

Stanley wasn't so sure. 'Grandad said that when he met Grandma, he just knew God wanted them to be together. Grandad didn't *do* anything in particular. He didn't *say* anything special. He just told God he really liked her and things started to fall into place.'

'And have you told God you really like Roselle?' Sparky asked.

'Of course I have,' Stanley replied. His voice was full of gloom. 'But nothing's fallen into place so far. She still doesn't even notice me.'

'She will,' said Sparky. 'If God wants you to marry Roselle, then nothing will keep you apart. Nothing in the whole world.'

'But what if He doesn't?'

'Well...' Sparky thought for a moment. 'Let's worry about that another time. For now, I think what you and Roselle really need is a little bit of a helping hand from me...'

* * * *

'**Eurgh!** What's that *awful* smell?'

It was Monday morning and Mrs Smart was running late for school. As usual, she was trying to do five different things at once. But, as Stanley walked into the kitchen with Sparky at his heels, she stopped doing all of them to sniff something nasty in the air.

'What *is* that?' She wrinkled not just her nose but her entire face. 'That's disgusting.'

Stanley's face turned deep red.

'It's not disgusting,' Sparky said. 'It's Stanley.'

Mrs Smart looked horrified. 'But why on earth do you smell so terrible, Stanley? What have you been doing? You stink!'

It wasn't anything Stanley had done. The first step in Sparky's plan to help Stanley win Roselle was to make him smell nice.

'Girls like it when boys smell nice,' she'd told him. 'Think about how Dad smells when he gets in from work. Horrid. Nobody wants to be around someone who smells like that.'

So Sparky had mixed up a special potion. 'When you wear this, Stanley,' she'd said, 'you'll smell nicer than all the other boys in the whole school.'

She'd fetched an empty bottle from the kitchen sink – it smelt a bit but that wouldn't matter, she'd said. Into it, Sparky had poured some of Mr Smart's aftershave lotion. She'd then added a few (quite a few) squirts of Mrs Smart's different perfumes.

Feeling that the potion wasn't smelly enough yet, she'd dribbled in some of Sissy's baby shampoo and some of Mrs Smart's bath oil too.

Then she'd remembered the oils Mrs Smart sometimes burnt in her oil burner to make the house smell nice. Sparky's favourite was 'clove' so she'd added the clove oil to the mix.

For the final touch, she'd grabbed a handful of rose

petals from the rose bush in the garden. These she'd crushed up and rolled together in her hands, and poked down into the bottle.

'Now all I need to do is shake it up,' she'd said.

'Erm... is it meant to be that colour?' Stanley had asked.

'The colour, Stanley, is neither here nor there,' Sparky had replied. (She'd never used this expression before but was very pleased to have the opportunity to use it in that moment.) 'What matters is the smell.' And she'd waved the bottle under Stanley's nose.

Stanley had breathed in – and begun to choke uncontrollably.

'Too strong!' he'd managed to splutter. 'That smell is way too strong! I'm not wearing that!'

'It's not too strong at all,' Sparky had replied. 'It's not as if you're going to be wearing the whole bottle. You just

splash a bit on like Dad does with his aftershave lotion.'

Stanley had refused to do any splashing, so Sparky had splashed it on for him.

'You'll thank me later,' she'd said.

Stanley didn't.

Mr Smart walked into the kitchen and stopped dead. 'What's that *awful* smell?' he demanded.

Stanley's face was already as red as it could go.

'It's *not* awful!' snapped Sparky. 'It's Stanley, and *I* think he smells lovely.'

'Morning all,' said Grandad. He'd let himself in through the front door, ready to walk Sparky to school.

In the kitchen doorway, he hesitated. 'What's that *awful* smell?' he asked.

'Right, that's it!' Stanley pushed past Grandad and ran upstairs to the bathroom. But even though he washed his face six times, until his skin felt sore and tight, he couldn't get rid of the smell completely. And by lunchtime, he'd come out in a rash all over his neck.

Not one to be easily put off, Sparky kept her ideas coming.

'I know what you should do, Stanley,' she said the next day. 'You should walk around school, whistling. People who whistle look cool and confident. Roselle is bound to notice you if you walk around whistling.'

Stanley made a face. 'I hate whistling. It hurts my ears. People who whistle are stupid. Anyway,' he added, 'I don't want Roselle to notice me now. I've got a rash all over my neck!'

'I know what you could do!' Another idea leapt into Sparky's brain. 'You could do lots of loud laughing.'

Stanley scratched his neck. 'Loud laughing at what?'

'I don't know – anything,' Sparky replied. 'Make it up. If Roselle sees you laughing a lot, she'll think you're just the sort of happy-go-lucky person she'd like to spend time with.'

Stanley looked anything but happy. 'I can't just walk around laughing,' he grumbled. 'Nobody just walks around laughing.'

Sparky shrugged her shoulders. 'Well, it's up to you. But what you've got to ask yourself is: how much do I want Roselle to like me?'

Two days later, at about half past eleven in the morning, Sparky had another idea.

It was always inconvenient when an idea came to her at school. Her teacher, Mr Barber, was telling the class about the time he'd won a baking competition with a pumpkin soufflé.

For some reason, this made Sparky think of Barbara, Grandad's purple and orange moped.

No sooner had Barbara popped into Sparky's head than everything else popped out of it. And she couldn't care two hoots about Mr Barber's pumpkin soufflé, no matter how much of a winner it was.

All she wanted was for the school day to be over so that she could talk to Grandad.

'Grandad! I need your help!' When the day was finally over, Sparky charged towards him as he waited for her by the school gate.

'Do you indeed?' said Grandad. 'Is it something I can do for you while we're walking home?'

'Oh, it's not for me,' Sparky replied. 'It's for Stanley.'

'It won't involve giving him another rash, I hope,' said Grandad.

Sparky's face looked a little put out. 'It wasn't my fault Stanley got a rash. How was I to know he had extra-delicate skin?'

'From the sounds of that potion you mixed up,' Grandad said, 'I think he got away quite lightly.'

'Anyway, Grandad' – Sparky was impatient to put her latest Roselle plan into action – 'I've had an idea.'

'Well, that's wonderful,' Grandad answered. 'Come on,

then, let's hear it.'

Sparky's eyes glowed. 'You know Stanley's in love with Roselle?'

'I had heard.' Grandad nodded.

'Here's what I think he should do.' Sparky's face beamed with pride. 'He should pretend he rides to school – **on a motorbike!**'

Grandad's bushy eyebrows did a little dance.

'If Roselle thinks Stanley rides a motorbike,' Sparky pressed on, 'she'll think he's really exciting and grown up. And she'll fall in love with him back, just like *that*.'

As she said 'just like *that*', Sparky tried to click her fingers. But finger-clicking was something she still hadn't mastered and all that came out was a soft, muffled sort of 'pffft'.

'I hate to point out the obvious,' said Grandad, 'but Stanley doesn't ride a motorbike.'

'Yes,' Sparky cried, 'but Roselle doesn't know that!'

'Stanley's not even old enough to ride a motorbike.'

'But Roselle might not know that either! All Stanley's got to do – and this is where you come in, Grandad – is walk into school carrying your spare moped helmet. He won't need to ride a motorbike or anything, but it'll *look* as if he rides one! Please can Stanley borrow the helmet, Grandad – *please*!'

Grandad's eyebrows settled back down and made his face look thoughtful.

'Isn't it just the best idea I've ever had?' Sparky wasn't quite sure why Grandad's feet weren't skipping with excitement the way hers were. But she knew that even

if this wasn't her best idea yet, it definitely had to be at least her second best.

'And what does Stanley think about this idea?' Grandad said finally.

'That's the best part!' Sparky almost shrieked. 'He doesn't know about it yet! But when he does – he's going to think I'm the genius to end all geniuses!'

'Hmm...' Grandad stroked his whiskery chin. 'Are you sure about that?'

'Well, why wouldn't he?' Sparky felt a tinge of disappointment. What was wrong with grown-ups? Why did they always seem to miss the point?

'Not wanting to be a wet blanket or anything, Sparky,'

Grandad said, 'but if Stanley pretends to Roselle that he rides a motorbike when he doesn't, that wouldn't be very honest. Would it?'

'But he wouldn't actually be saying, "Look at me, I ride a motorbike",' Sparky insisted. 'That's just what Roselle would *think* if he turned up at school with your spare helmet. That's why it's such a clever idea!'

Grandad shook his head. 'It's still a lie, though, Sparky. And I don't think Stanley would want his friendship with Roselle to be based on a lie, do you?'

Sparky's feet had stopped skipping. She wished she'd kept her idea to herself until she'd seen Stanley.

'If this is because you don't want Stanley to borrow your spare helmet, then fine,' she said. 'I'll find him a helmet from somewhere else.'

Grandad smiled. 'It's nothing to do with borrowing the helmet, Sparky. What's mine is yours, you know that.' Grandad put an arm round Sparky's shoulder. 'It's just that God wants us to care for our friends and love them, doesn't He? And you can't love and care for someone if you're not being honest with them. God doesn't like lies, Sparky,' he added. 'Lies aren't the way to get what you want.'

Sparky wasn't going to be put off. 'But what if it's a helpful sort of lie?' she asked. 'This helmet plan would be *so* helpful to Stanley. And if Roselle liked Stanley back, he'd be really happy. God would want Stanley to be really happy, wouldn't He?'

'Of course He would,' Grandad replied. 'But lies don't make people happy. Not in the end. Lying isn't good for us. That's why God tells us not to do it.'

They walked on in silence.

When they reached the pelican crossing, they waited for the little green man to appear and the pipping to start. Sparky always thought it would be much more interesting if pelican crossings played music rather than pipping at you madly. If they played songs loudly, you'd still know it was time to cross the road *and* you could sing along as you went.

'I know you only want to help, Sparky,' Grandad said, once they were safely on the other side. 'But it's important to help Stanley in the right way. In any case,' he added, 'what's the hurry? Stanley's not going anywhere and as far as we know, neither is Roselle. If you really want to help' – they turned into Priory Park and one of Miss Clatworthy's cats shot out of a bush in front of them. Grandad nearly tripped over it – 'if you really want to help, why not get together with Stanley and have a chat with God about it? Ask God what He thinks. If you're doing what God wants, you can't go far wrong.'

Sparky looked at Grandad. For some reason, she hadn't thought of talking to God about Roselle – with Stanley or without him. She'd been too full of her own ideas.

'Everything about us matters to God,' Grandad says. 'Hopes, dreams, friendships...'

'Who you're going to marry,' Sparky added.

Grandad chuckled. 'Well, yes. But I don't think Stanley needs to worry about that quite yet.'

He might do, Sparky thought, *if Roselle's the one*. But she kept the thought to herself.

✲ ✲ ✲ ✲

'There's something we need to do, Stanley,' Sparky said when Stanley got home from school. 'It's *very* urgent.'

Stanley knew that when Sparky said something was *very* urgent, it probably wasn't urgent at all. He put his bag down in the hall and walked past her into the kitchen.

Sparky followed. 'Didn't you hear me?' she said. 'I said it's *very* urgent.'

'What's *very* urgent is that I'm hungry and thirsty,' mumbled Stanley, as he marched to the fridge.

'How's Roselle?' Sparky asked.

Stanley spun round. '**Sssh!**' he hissed. 'I don't want everyone knowing about her.'

Sparky looked round. 'There's no one else in here.'

'Walls have ears, Sparky. Walls and windows and doors.'

Sparky blinked at him. 'Do they?' The oddest picture of a house covered in ears jumped into her head.

Stanley raised his eyes. 'Of course they do! Don't you know anything?'

Sparky knew for a fact that walls, windows and doors didn't have ears. (You're sure to know that too. You'll also probably know that what Stanley meant was, 'Shush! There might not be anyone else in the kitchen but someone still might hear us.')

'In that case,' Sparky said, and she lowered her voice, 'meet me in my room in five minutes and we can talk in private.'

Before Stanley had the chance to argue, Sparky shot out of the kitchen and ran upstairs.

Unfortunately, there was nothing private about Sparky's room. Sissy was in there (well, it was her room too). Mrs Smart was also there, sitting on the bed trying to comb a toffee out of Sissy's hair.

Sparky could see they'd both be there for a while. The toffee wasn't going anywhere anytime soon.

She darted back down to the kitchen. 'Change of plan, Stanley,' she whispered. 'Meet me in *your* room in five minutes instead.'

'I don't want you in my room!' Stanley said. Sparky had already disappeared.

When Stanley finally joined her, Sparky was quick to close his bedroom door behind him.

'Listen, Stanley,' she said. 'We don't ever have to say the name "Roselle" out loud.' She was careful to mouth the name 'Roselle' rather than speak it. 'We can just say "R". Then no one will know who we're talking about. Neither will the walls or the windows or the doors.'

Stanley's face frowned. 'We don't have to say her name at all,' he said. 'There's no reason to talk about her.'

'But there is, Stanley,' Sparky insisted. 'We need to talk about her with God.'

'Why?'

'Because everything matters to God, Stanley. Hopes, dreams, friendships – *and* who you're going to marry.'

Stanley stared at his sister through narrowed eyes. 'Have you been talking to Grandad?'

'No... Maybe... Possibly.' Sparky dropped down onto Stanley's bed. 'Anyway, it doesn't matter. What's important is that we ask God to help.'

Stanley's eyebrows did a puzzled shuffle. 'Help with what?'

'With making "R" fall in love with you – what do you think?!' Sometimes brothers could be very silly. 'And the sooner the better if you ask me. Maybe even by this weekend.'

Stanley shook his head. 'Not this weekend. "R" won't be here. She's going away with her parents. She's a bit annoyed too because her cousins were supposed to be looking after her hamster but now they're not going to.'

'She told you that?' Sparky jumped up and clapped her hands. 'This is brilliant – you've actually spoken to her!'

'No,' Stanley answered. 'I heard her telling someone else. And I've got homework to do now, so could you leave my room, please?'

As Stanley opened his door and waited for his sister to leave, his words about the hamster suddenly exploded inside Sparky's brain.

'But this is it! This is *it*, Stanley!' And Sparky slammed the door shut again.

'Can you *not* slam the doors, please!' Mrs Smart shouted from Sparky's bedroom. 'I've got a toffee emergency on my hands – I don't want a broken door as well!'

Sparky would have called, 'Sorry!' but she was too excited.

'What are you talking about?' Stanley asked. 'What's *it*?'

Sparky stared at him. Sometimes she had to ask herself how it was possible that Stanley was her brother. He seemed to have no powers of quick-thinking, while her brain was one massive, quick-thinking ball of ideas. All the time.

'It's perfect!' she cried. 'Totally and completely perfectly perfect!'

Stanley was so confused his eyebrows didn't seem to know where to put themselves.

Sparky stood in front of him, hands behind her back and a triumphant gleam in her eye.

'Get ready for the idea of the century!' she announced. 'You, Stanley Smart, are going to look after "R's" hamster...'

* * * *

The Smarts had never owned a hamster. They'd never owned any pets. Although Sparky sometimes wondered if they did partly own Miss Clatworthy's cats, Monday, Tuesday and Thursday.

Monday, Tuesday and especially Thursday seemed to think the Smarts' garden belonged to them. They spent far more time in it than they did in their own. They left far more poo in the Smarts' garden than they did in their own too.

'But we don't know how to look after a hamster,' Stanley had said, immediately after Sparky's latest idea had **leapt** out of her brain.

Mrs Smart had said so too, even when Sparky had told her how important this was to Stanley. 'We don't know how to look after a hamster. Anyway, I don't like the way their faces swell up.'

'Their faces don't swell up, Mum,' Sparky had replied. 'They just look big and nobbly when they've got food in their pouches.'

Mrs Smart had looked horrified. 'They've got pouches

in their faces?'

'Oh, yes,' Sparky had said. 'I looked it up. I found some gorgeous hamster pictures too. Would you like to see them? I saved them all on Stanley's computer.'

Mrs Smart shook her head. 'I think I'll give them a miss, thanks all the same.'

'*Please*, Mum,' Sparky begged. 'Hamsters are the best! It's only for a weekend. And I'll bet you a million pounds that if we have this one to stay, you'll end up loving it!'

'Sparky, you don't have a million pounds,' said Mrs Smart.

'Well, not yet, but one day I might. Go on... *please*?'

Mrs Smart sighed. 'Oh, all right,' she agreed at last. 'But it stays in its cage, do you hear me? You don't let it out, even for a minute.'

Before Roselle's hamster was delivered to the Smarts' house on Friday evening, Sparky was fairly sure she knew just about everything there was to know about keeping hamsters.

'And just think, Stanley,' she said to the back of Stanley's head. Stanley wouldn't move from the lounge window. He wanted to be the first to see Roselle and her hamster arrive. 'After this, Roselle will never ask her cousins to look after her hamster again – because she'll have you to ask instead. **And I reckon that means you're practically engaged!**'

A car pulled into the driveway.

'Oh, no...' Stanley murmured. 'They're here.' He quickly licked the palms of his hands and used them to smooth his hair down.

'There's nothing to worry about, Stanley,' said Sparky.

'This is the best idea ever. And your hair looks fantastic by the way.'

Stanley's cheeks glowed pink.

Mr Smart got to the front door first. 'Do come in,' he said.

Stanley and Sparky appeared in the hall behind him.

Roselle's dad stood on the front step. He held the hamster cage in front of him. It was quite a big cage and Roselle's dad was quite short. Which made the cage look even bigger.

'No, no, I mustn't stop,' Roselle's dad said. 'Got to go and pick Roselle up from her dance class. We've got an early start tomorrow.'

'Right,' replied Mr Smart. 'Then I'll just take that, shall I?'

He reached out his arms and Roselle's dad placed the hamster cage into them. The cage didn't look as big when

Mr Smart held it.

'It's all nice and clean, ready for you.' Roselle's dad glanced at Stanley. 'You must be Simon,' he said. 'It's very kind of you to offer to look after Roselle's hamster, I must say. I've never heard Roselle mention you before.'

Stanley's shoulders sank a little. 'Erm... actually, it's Stanley,' he muttered.

Roselle's dad didn't answer.

Sparky asked, 'So Roselle didn't come with you, then?'

Roselle's dad shook his head.

Stanley's shoulders sank further.

'What's his name?' Mr Smart asked, with a nod towards the hamster cage.

'Reggie,' Roselle's dad replied. 'Well, his full name is Reginald Montgomery Alphonzo the Third. Bit of a mouthful, I know, but Roselle insisted. I just call him Reggie. To be honest,' he went on, 'hamsters don't need looking after if you're only going away for a weekend. They store food so they're not going to go hungry if no one's there for a couple of days. But,' he added, 'Roselle insisted, so here he is.'

Mr Smart peered into the cage. Reginald Montgomery Alphonzo the Third wasn't anywhere in sight.

'You won't see him,' Roselle's dad went on. 'Spends all day asleep buried in his little cubbyhole. Spends half the night asleep too, as far as I can make out. To be honest, I'm not really sure why people keep hamsters as pets. I mean, it's not like having a dog, is it? You can do things with a dog. Still, Roselle insisted.'

He reached into the pocket of his jacket and pulled out

a small plastic box. He held it out. 'There's more food in here,' he said, 'but you won't need it.'

As Mr Smart's hands were full of cage, Stanley stepped forward and took the box.

'Anyway, Simon, thanks again,' Roselle's dad said to Stanley. 'I'll pop back for him on Sunday evening.'

'Will Roselle come with you then?' Sparky asked.

'Doubt it. Roselle likes to have a long bath on a Sunday evening. If it was up to me, we wouldn't have a bath. Just a shower. Showers are far more economical. But we've kept it. Roselle insisted.'

Roselle's dad stepped towards his car. 'Ooh, there is one other thing. I don't know if Roselle mentioned this, Simon, but Reggie is quite an escape artist. One minute you think he's in his cage, the next... well, he could be anywhere. Anyway, have fun. See you on Sunday night.'

And he was gone.

At bedtime, Stanley said, 'Do you think we ought to have a look for Reggie in his cubbyhole? Just to make sure he's all right?'

Mr and Mrs Smart, Sparky and Stanley were all gathered round the cage.

'Oh, no,' Mrs Smart replied. 'Don't disturb him. If we're really lucky, perhaps he'll sleep right through till Sunday evening. Then I won't have to listen to him running about... or nibbling... or scratching himself.' She shuddered.

'Hamsters are lovely, Mum,' Sparky said. 'I don't know why you don't like them.'

'Because they look like mice with swollen faces,' Mrs Smart replied.

Sparky laughed. 'No, they don't!'

Mrs Smart was in no mood for laughter. 'They do to me.'

When Stanley went upstairs to get ready for bed, Sparky followed him.

'I'm sorry Roselle didn't come with her dad,' she said. 'Her dance class must have been very important. Perhaps she's getting ready for an exam or something.'

'Or something,' Stanley grunted.

'She'll probably come over on Sunday,' Sparky added. 'She'll want to say thank you.'

Stanley wasn't so sure.

'And even if she doesn't' – Sparky was determined to cheer him up – 'you'll see her at school on Monday, so you'll be able to have long chats with her about Reggie then.'

Stanley couldn't imagine having long chats with Roselle about anything.

'Looking after Roselle's hamster is still the *best* idea, isn't it?' Sparky said.

Stanley went into the bathroom and closed the door.

✯ ✯ ✯ ✯

No one except Sissy slept well that night.

Stanley lay awake because he couldn't stop wondering if Roselle's dance class was the only reason she hadn't come to his house; or if, actually, she hated him.

Sparky lay awake because she was disappointed. She'd been looking forward to meeting Roselle. She wanted to tell her what a marvellous brother Stanley was, which meant he was bound to make a marvellous husband.

Mrs Smart lay awake because she couldn't believe a swollen-faced mouse-creature was sleeping in her lounge. How could she have let this happen?

Mr Smart lay awake because Mrs Smart lay awake. Whenever Mrs Smart lay awake, she made sure he was awake too.

Stanley spent most of the next day on the sofa, staring into Reggie's cage. He only moved to get something to eat or drink from the kitchen. Then he went straight back to the lounge.

'I don't think you have to spend all day staring at Reggie's cage,' Sparky said. 'I think hamsters pretty much do their own thing whether we stare at their cages or not.'

But Stanley wouldn't move. 'If I'm going to look after this hamster, I'm going to look after it properly,' he said. 'Roselle hates me already. I don't want her to hate me even more.'

When it was time to go to bed again, there was still no sign of Reginald Montgomery Alphonzo the Third.

There was no sign of him on Sunday morning either. His food and water hadn't been touched. Nothing in the cage looked any different from the night before.

When the Smarts went to church, Stanley wanted to take Reggie with them.

'I could sit at the back with the cage,' he said. 'No one would know.'

'I'd know, Stanley,' said Mrs Smart.

It wasn't until four o'clock in the afternoon, when the

Smarts were all back at Priory Park, that Stanley began to worry. Surely he should have had a glimpse of Reggie by now. At the very least he should have heard him.

'Roselle's dad says he likes to hide away in his cubbyhole,' Mr Smart reminded him. 'He's just doing what hamsters do.'

'And he probably popped out in the night,' added Sparky. 'Night time's when hamsters mostly come out.'

Another half an hour went by – and Stanley couldn't bear it any longer.

'I'm looking in Reggie's cubbyhole,' he said.

'No, Stanley!' replied Sparky. 'Don't disturb him. He's probably tired – what with coming to stay in a new place and everything.'

Stanley shook his head. 'Roselle's dad will be coming to pick him up soon. I've got to check he's all right.'

'Of course he's all right,' Sparky said. 'Why wouldn't he be?'

Mrs Smart had been hoping for a quiet end to the weekend. She didn't particularly enjoy Monday mornings and going back to school. This term had already felt very long and there were several weeks to go before the holidays. As much as she loved children, on Monday mornings Mrs Smart often wished she could stay at home.

So, the last thing she wanted to hear as she sat in the kitchen with a cup of tea was Stanley's desperate shriek: 'Reggie's gone!'

'Don't be daft, Stanley,' said Mr Smart. He marched into the lounge. 'He can't be gone.'

'What do you mean "gone"?' gasped Mrs Smart. She

hurried in after Mr Smart, Sissy hanging on to the hem of her jumper.

'He's gone!' Stanley squealed.

Stanley didn't normally squeal. But at this moment, he was so overcome by the horror of the empty hamster cage that he couldn't speak without sounding squealy.

'Let me see.' Mr Smart moved Stanley out of the way and leaned over the cage. He pulled Reggie's cubbyhole out from its corner and prodded in the bedding with his fingers.

There definitely wasn't a hamster in there.

He peered all around the cage – in the play tube; in the hamster wheel. He even flicked the sawdust about, although Reggie couldn't possibly be hiding under there. Not unless he was a very flat hamster.

He glanced at Mrs Smart. 'Reggie's gone.'

'That's what I've been trying to tell you!' Stanley had to fight with himself not to burst into tears.

'*What?*' Mrs Smart turned pale (although not as pale as Stanley).

Mr Smart's eyes darted round the room. 'Roselle's dad did say Reggie was a bit of an escape artist.'

'*A bit of an escape artist?*' Mrs Smart was beside herself. 'Are you telling me there's a swollen-faced mouse-creature on the loose in this house?' She jumped up on the sofa, pulling Sissy with her.

Sparky shook her head. 'He won't be swollen-faced. Not unless he's got food in his pouches,' she said helpfully.

'I don't care!' Mrs Smart cried. 'You've got to find him – now!'

'He won't do any harm,' Sparky said. 'He'll probably just find a dark corner somewhere and go to sleep.'

Sparky had turned a little pale herself. This wasn't in the plan. If Stanley had managed to lose Roselle's hamster the first time he'd looked after him for her, chances are, she wouldn't want to marry him.

'Phone Grandad,' Mrs Smart whimpered.

'Why?' asked Mr Smart.

'Because he'll know what to do,' Mrs Smart snapped. 'Tell him we need him and we need him now!'

In less than ten minutes, Grandad was at the front door, accompanied by his friend from down the road, Verity Pringle.

'We were just about to have a teacake,' Grandad said. 'What's the big emergency?'

'Eggy on,' announced Sissy.

Understandably, Grandad looked confused.

'Reggie's gone,' Sparky said.

Grandad's only advice was to hunt for Reggie, which most of the Smarts were already doing. *Most* because Mrs Smart refused to leave the sofa. She wouldn't let Sissy leave it either.

'What if it runs up my trouser leg?' she said. 'What if it attacks me? Rats do that, you know. They attack people!'

Nobody bothered to point out that Reggie was hardly a rat. They were too busy hunting for him.

At least Grandad and Mrs Pringle could hunt too. The more hunters, the more likelihood of finding the escaped hamster.

They all searched every dark corner.

Grandad and Mr Smart pulled things out of cupboards

and peered under furniture.

Mrs Pringle went right through the dirty washing in the laundry basket and the clean washing in the airing cupboard.

Sparky and Stanley slid books out of the bookshelves.

When Sparky noticed Grandad searching through a cupboard on his own in the kitchen, she scurried over to him.

'Grandad?' she whispered. 'Looking after Reggie for Roselle *was* a good idea, wasn't it?'

Grandad wasn't sure how to answer, since Reggie was clearly missing. 'It was certainly a very kind thought,' he said.

Sparky whispered, 'And it was honest and it wasn't a lie or anything, was it, Grandad?'

'No. As I say, it was very kind.'

'Then God will help us find Reggie, won't He? He won't want Reggie to be lost and He won't want Roselle not to marry Stanley.'

Grandad smiled. 'You mustn't worry about who Stanley's going to marry, Sparky. God's not worrying about it. All God wants is for us to put Him first – talk to Him about everything, include Him in everything and do what He'd want us to do – and He'll work the rest out in His own good time. In His own God time, in fact.'

Mrs Pringle appeared in the doorway. 'You know what's odd?' she said.

'What's that?' asked Grandad.

'Droppings,' replied Mrs Pringle.

'Sorry?' said Mr Smart. He walked into the kitchen holding a screwdriver. He'd just taken the side of the bath off to check Reggie hadn't found a way in underneath. He hadn't.

Unfortunately, he now couldn't put the bath back together.

'Droppings,' Mrs Pringle repeated.

Mr Smart looked puzzled. 'No, sorry, I don't follow.'

'Ah, clever.' Grandad nodded knowingly.

'I've looked all over this house and there aren't any hamster droppings,' Mrs Pringle explained. 'About a year ago, I had mice in my kitchen. They must have found a way in from the garden. I didn't see them, but I knew they were there – because of the droppings.'

Sparky took this in for a moment. 'So you're saying that, if there aren't any hamster droppings, there can't be a hamster loose in the house.'

'I think it's very unlikely,' Mrs Pringle replied.

Stanley darted into the lounge. 'There aren't any droppings in the cage either,' he called. 'It's just as clean as when Roselle's dad dropped it off.'

'Now, that is odd,' said Mrs Pringle.

'Maybe you can get a special type of hamster,' Sparky suggested. 'You know – one that doesn't do droppings.'

'I rather doubt it,' said Grandad.

'I don't care what type of hamster it is,' wailed Mrs Smart. '**I just wish you'd find it!**'

Stanley flopped onto the floor. 'I wish we could find him too,' he moaned. 'What am I going to do? Roselle's dad will be here soon. I'll have to tell him I've lost her hamster. That there's just no sign of him. It's as if...' Stanley's face crumpled a little. 'It's as if Reggie was never even here...'

Sparky dropped down next to him. 'I'll tell him, Stanley.' She put her arm round him. 'This is all my fault – it was all my idea. But Grandad says God will work everything out in His own good time. In His own God time, in fact. So you don't have to worry if Roselle doesn't want to marry you anymore, because I'm sure God will find you someone else who will.'

Mrs Smart shook her head. 'Sorry, am I missing something here? Roselle wants to *marry* you?'

Before Sparky could try to explain, the front doorbell rang.

'Oh, no,' Stanley groaned. 'I'm done for. I'll never be able to look at Roselle again. I'll never be able to look at *anyone* again.'

Because Mrs Smart still refused to move from her standing position on the sofa, Mr Smart went to answer the door.

'I'm coming with you,' said Sparky.

'I'm not,' mumbled Stanley.

Roselle's dad stood on the doorstep.

'Hello,' he said. 'Only me again.'

There was no sign of Roselle.

'Hello,' said Mr Smart. 'How was your weekend away?'

'Terrific!' replied Roselle's dad. 'How's everything been here?'

'Wonderful,' said Mr Smart. He didn't quite know how to break the news.

Roselle's dad smiled. 'Excellent.' He didn't seem to know what to say next either.

'Is Roselle having her long bath?' Sparky asked.

'She is, yes,' Roselle's dad answered. 'Every Sunday night. I did tell her she didn't really need a bath. She had a shower right before we left to come home. But, Roselle insisted.'

There was an awkward pause.

Then, 'The thing is –' Mr Smart and Roselle's dad spoke at the same time.

'Sorry – you first.' They said that at the same time too.

Mr Smart smiled and drew his thumb and forefinger across his lips, as if he was zipping up his mouth. He then pointed at Roselle's dad to go first.

'The thing is…' Roselle's dad slowly began, 'this is really rather awkward.'

'What is?' asked Mr Smart.

Roselle's dad cleared his throat. 'I expect you've had a very quiet weekend with Reggie.'

'Erm… yes.' Mr Smart cleared his throat too. 'We haven't heard a peep from him the whole time.'

Roselle's dad nodded. 'I don't suppose you've seen him either, have you?'

Mr Smart was just about to reply that, no, they hadn't seen him and not only that, they had no idea where he was, when Roselle's dad blurted out: **'It's all my fault!'**

Sparky's eyebrows jumped together in a frown. 'What's your fault?'

'You see, I wasn't going to clean the cage out on Friday,' he went on. 'I only cleaned it out on Thursday so I didn't see the point. But, Roselle insisted. And while I was cleaning it out... well... the little blighter must have escaped.'

He'd hardly finished speaking when Stanley appeared in the hall.

Roselle's dad gave him a nod. 'All right, Simon? Anyway' – he cleared his throat for the second time – 'the first thing we saw when we got back this evening was Reginald Montgomery Alphonzo the Third, sitting in the middle of the hall, large as life, eating a peanut. I mean, eating a peanut – can you believe it!'

Stanley took a step closer. 'You mean, Reggie was never here in the first place? He's been running around your house all by himself all weekend?'

'It would seem so, Simon.' Roselle's dad looked very apologetic. 'So what you've been looking after is, in actual fact, just an empty cage.'

Stanley could have hugged him. He didn't (which was probably just as well) – but he could have.

* * * *

When Stanley went up to bed later that evening, he found Sparky waiting for him in his room.

'I hope this isn't going to become a habit, Sparky,' he said.

'I just wanted to say, Stanley,' she began, 'that from now on, I'm going to keep my nose out of your business.'

'I'll believe that when it happens,' Stanley said.

'No, I mean it. The only nose that belongs in your business is God's. And not because He's being nosey or busy-bodying or anything, but because He cares about you.'

'I know that,' Stanley replied.

'I care about you too, Stanley,' Sparky went on. 'That's why I tried to help. But I shouldn't have tried to make Roselle want to marry you. Who you marry is up to God, not me.'

'Everything's up to God, not us,' said Stanley, 'as long as we let Him be in charge.'

'And do things His way and not ours,' Sparky added. 'Which is hard for me sometimes because I have so many good ideas.'

'God understands that, though. He made you with a quick-thinking brain.' Stanley kicked off his slippers. 'Can I get ready for bed now, please?'

'Of course you can, Stanley.'

Sparky headed for his bedroom door. As she stepped through, she turned. 'But if by any chance you do still want to marry Roselle, I'm sure there's *something* I can do to help.'

'Goodnight, Sparky,' Stanley said.

He reached out and shut the door, with Sparky safely on the other side.

Join the Smart family and the other residents of Priory Park for more fun!

THE CRINKLY COUSINS AND OTHER MISHAPS
ISBN 9781838581497

THE PURRING WOMBAT AND OTHER MISADVENTURES
ISBN 9781838581503

THE WRONG TOILET AND OTHER DISASTERS
ISBN 9781838581510

THE SCHOOL FETE FIASCO AND OTHER CALAMITIES
ISBN 9781838581527

SHIPWRECKED AT THE LIBRARY AND OTHER EXPLOITS
ISBN 9781838581534

GRANDAD JELLY LEGS AND OTHER ESCAPADES
ISBN 9781838581541

All of the books in the **Spark Smart from Priory Park** series are available from **kevinmayhew.com** or from your local Christian bookshop